MICRO-MACRO DISCIPLING

Rediscovering the Way of Kingdom Growth

Becoming a Change-Agent with Jesus

SILAS NG

Foreword by Eddie Gibbs, Philemon Choi,
and Terry Walling

HIS Publishing Group
4310 Wiley Post Rd., Suite 201D
Addison, TX 75001
info@hispub.com

Unless otherwise noted Scriptures are taken from *New Revised Standard Version*. All rights reserved worldwide.

Library of Congress Control Number: 2018905117
ISBN: 978-1-7753428-0-9 *paperback*
          978-1-7753428-1-6 *electronic*

Printed in Canada

HISPUBLISHING
GROUP
Division of Human Improvement Specialists, llc.
www.hispubg.com | *info@hispubg.com*

DEDICATIONS

To my wife Michelle, our elder son Ignatius, his wife Anna and their daughter
Zoe Glory, and Athanasius, our younger son, who always encourages me to follow Jesus as a faithful disciple
and to
my seven spiritual fathers and coaches,

Dr. Philemon Choi
Professor Rev. Dr. Eddie Gibbs
Dr. Sai Kui Lee
Professor Rev. Dr. Gil Stieglitz
Rev. Dr. John Stott
Professor Rev. Dr. Terry Walling
Most Rev. Yong Ping Chung

Through their mentoring I have become a better disciple of Christ to live out the
parable of the growing seed to extend
His Kingdom.

ACKNOWLEDGMENTS

Thanks to Dr. Eddie Gibbs, Dr. Philemon Choi, and Dr. Terry Walling for writing the foreword. Thanks also to Ms. Kristie Savage for editing, to Lillian Mak, Liel Yim, and Doreen Yim, who helped as a research team, and to Eric Lee, who designed the front and back cover of this book.

FOREWORD

By Eddie Gibbs

Much has been said and written on the urgent and widespread need for disciple making in our twenty-first century context. How do we translate and interpret Jesus' mission priority to go into all the world and make disciples in today's world, when churches throughout the Western world have neglected and failed to understand this mission mandate? It is no wonder that the "Great Commission" has become the "Great Omission," and the prevailing strategy has become "come to church" rather than "go into all the world." Outreach has been replaced by in-drag.

Such a radical change of strategy has resulted in church growth becoming little more than the re-cycling of the saints, with churches growing at the expense of others. In the absence of a clear understanding of the nature of discipleship, we have resorted to consumer church, in which church attendees expect to be entertained and their expectations catered to.

Such is the daunting challenge that Bishop Silas Ng is bravely addressing. It is one thing to describe the nature of authentic discipleship and to search for examples of churches that are seeking ways of turning decisions for Christ into disciples of Christ. It is quite another to move from conceptualizer and commentator to becoming a change-agent, beginning with oneself, and developing an effective long-term, step-by-step strategy to bring about deep-level, sustained transformation.

Bishop Silas' book is an honest account of the methodical steps he has taken to implement his God-given vision. His is a personal journey, starting with his own frustrations in coming to terms with discipleship based on an intimate relationship with his Lord and Savior, Jesus Christ, and openness to the empowering and guidance of the Holy Spirit.

His journey was further enriched by his doctoral studies at Fuller Seminary, with the extensive reading required, insights gained from lectures, his interaction with fellow students, and his consultation with church leaders and mentors. He developed research and ongoing assessment tools. He provided a daily, devotional blog so that countless numbers of disciples-in-training could accompany him on his journey. He also led seminars and scheduled leadership conferences to help in the formation of disciple-making leaders.

"Micro-Macro Discipleship" is a work in progress, as Bishop Silas Ng would be the first to admit. This book will bring a wider awareness of the work being undertaken, and hopefully it will inspire others to undertake their own journeys into discipleship and invite others to accompany them. After all, this is what Jesus intended at the outset!

Dr. Eddie Gibbs
Professor Emeritus
School of Intercultural Studies
Fuller Theological Seminary
Pasadena, California

FOREWORD

BY PHILEMON CHOI

The theme of this thought provoking and soul-searching book touched my heart: "Micro-Macro Discipling – Rediscovering Jesus' way of Kingdom Growth."

Bishop Silas and I had been blessed by the same mentor: Rev. Dr. John Stott. Rev. Stott's words, "growth without depth," captured such an insightful observation of the global church's crisis: lack of depth in discipling and understanding the meaning of becoming "radical disciples of Jesus Christ."

Silas' discovery that only 10% of Christians have daily devotion is an alarming fact. Daily devotion is central to the spiritual growth of a Christian—being nurtured by the Word of God, connected to the love of our Father through prayer with the Holy Spirit, and becoming like Christ—day by day, moment by moment. This is the core objective of micro-discipling.

Silas is sincere and honest in sharing his own struggle to sustain a daily intimate relationship with Christ. He conducted extensive research to discover the root of the crisis of why "The Great Commission" had become a "Great Omission."

Silas shares in a personal, soulful way how to do daily devotion through the web. That enabled Silas to touch many Christians who needed personal guidance as they endeavored to sustain their daily devotion.

When I visited Silas in Vancouver, I met Christians who were learning and practicing daily devotion with him. Then I discovered that he also mentored them on a personal basis, touching their lives in a loving way.

Discipling cannot be reduced to classroom-style information sharing; it has to be relational, rooted deeply in the word of God, and facilitated by the presence of the Holy Spirit.

Macro-discipling is a further step: reaching out to share God's love and His word with people outside of the church. The Great Commission is a command to "go" and reach all nations and all people with the holistic gospel of Jesus Christ—blessing all people around the world. Discipling is missional: building a community of missional disciples of Christ, locally and globally.

This book inspires every Christian to rethink the deeper meaning of becoming a disciple of Christ, and to learn how to mature in Christ and become a discipler for Christ. May this book reach more Christians, not only among the Chinese churches, but also touching lives in other parts of the global church of Christ.

Dr. Philemon Choi
Founder, Breakthrough Ltd.
President, Youth Global Network Ltd.

FOREWORD

By Terry B. Walling

In the age of information, transformed lives are front and center at the core need for the Church today.

If more information and more knowledge were the key to a different Church, we would have experienced revival years ago. We have the books. We are missing the disciples. The swing back to discipleship today seeks to respond to this need, re-building authentic life back into a Church. For years we focused on attracting people to worship services.

But many continue to see discipleship as an issue of more information. We are finding new ways to dispense re-packaged information using the latest app or recruiting people to watch teaching videos playing at today's multi-site church.

At its core, discipleship is a relationship between us and Christ.

There was never a time when Christ stopped relating to and discipling the disciples. There is never a time when Jesus is not discipling each of us. Discipleship happens every day, is for every Christ-follower, and is sourced in the Word and prayer.

Bishop Silas Ng takes discipleship all the way back to the very essence of an ongoing, daily, focused time with Christ. It is relationship fueled by breaking bread and intimate communication, producing a DNA and life that begins to germinate into new disciples, new churches, and new authentic life for the Church.

What makes Bishop Silas' book different is that it documents his journey back to the essence of discipleship, offering his personal journey and experiences in micro-discipleship (daily devotion). But it also provides compelling evidence and research that reveals what the micro-level of discipleship is missing from the behavior of the people of the church, thereby short-circuiting what is the source of authentic disciples.

You may need to ask yourself as you read this book, as I did, how long has it been since I have been with Jesus on a daily basis?

If that is your first response, even before what this work means for the church you lead or attend, then it has begun . . . a revolution of new life within, that as it germinates yields a harvest of disciples making disciples, and an authentic Church.

Dr. Terry Walling
President, Leader Breakthru
Professor, Fuller Theological Seminary, DMin Mentoring

PREFACE

The early Church received Jesus' secret of Kingdom growth and they grew exponentially. This is a book to tell you how Jesus' way of Kingdom growth is being re-discovered – Micro-Macro Discipling.

We are living in a connected world, a digital cyberspace, sending out messages, images, and video in the timeframe of a split second through all kinds of smart devices.

But many people live disconnected lives! Most people do not feel their lives are full of meaning.

Connected world but disconnected lives. Why?

I have been a pastor for almost thirty years. I myself had been living a disconnected life – burying myself in busyness, brokenness, and at the brink of burning out. Some years ago, I came to my senses, like the prodigal son in Jesus' parable.

This is a story of how Jesus led me to a more connected life. This is my story of how Jesus has given me this vision of Micro-Macro Discipling to help thousands of people around the world live more connected lives.

I am going to tell you a strategic plan for life with a track record that proves it works. This book contains three major sections, each of which describes the plan: research-based, theologically grounded, and strategically planned.

Part One ("Research-Based") explores contextual issues through interviews of some important Christian leaders and the results of a questionnaire completed by 1,179 Christians in 46 churches. The findings support my theory of the reality that fewer than 10 percent of Christians have a daily devotional time, which is directly related to the rationale for launching this Micro-Macro Discipling.

Part Two ("Theologically Grounded") describes the biblical, ecclesiological, and theological assumptions that serve as the foundation of the strategy. This section attempts to clarify the goal of the process by asking three simple but basic questions:

Why are fewer than 10 percent of Christians having a daily devotional time?
Is this a problem?
If so, how do church leaders deal with this problem?

A theology of Micro-Macro Discipling is explored and proposed, highlighting biblical teachings regarding the necessity and nature of this strategy.

Part Three ("Strategically Planned") provides a practical mentoring discipleship plan by outlining the tasks of a two-stage simple and gradual mentoring discipleship process. The heart of the proposed strategy is simple, focused, and deep – it seeks the development of a lifestyle that Jesus asked His disciples to live out two thousand years ago, and one that He continues to ask disciples to live out today.

CONTENTS

INTRODUCTION

The current church culture in North America is on life support. It is living off the work, money and energy of previous generations from a previous world order. The plug will be pulled either when the money runs out (80 percent of money given to congregations comes from people aged fifty-five and older) or when the remaining three-fourths of a generation who are institutional loyalists die off or both.

—Reggie McNeal, *The Present Future*

The inherited denominations are all in serious decline. Growing churches, whether denominational or independent, are bucking the trend largely as a result of transfer growth or, to a lesser extent, through the renewed participation of the lapsed. The widespread nature of decline across the ecclesial and theological spectrum and over the same time span indicates that the root causes of the slump are not primarily within the life of religious institution. Rather, they relate to a broader issues arising from their cultural context.

—Eddie Gibbs, *Church Morph*

What Is Micro-Macro Discipling?

Reggie McNeal and Eddie Gibbs point out the reality of the collapse of church culture and the serious decline of the inherited denominations. This decline addresses the question of why discipleship is a crucial issue. Indeed, as Gibbs explains, it relates to a broader issue arising from their cultural context and to the root that caused this decline. This leads to the next question: What is this root? John Stott names this root in three words: "growth without depth." He writes, "When I was traveling in the 1990s in the interests of the Langham Partnership International, I would often ask an audience how they would summarize the Christian scene in the world today. I would receive a variety of answers. But when invited to give my own answer to the question, I would sum it up in just three words, namely 'growth without depth.'"[1]

A short while ago I had dinner with one of the most respected Christian leaders in Hong Kong, Dr. Philemon Choi. He told me that every time he was with his mentor, Rev. Dr. John Stott, he was told that the biggest problem in church nowadays is exactly these three words: "growth without depth." Greg Ogden comments on this point, quoting John Stott: "For many years, 25 or more, the church-growth school has been dominant. I rejoice in the statistics, but we must say it is growth without depth. I believe it was Chuck Colson who said the church is 3,000 miles wide and an inch deep. Many are babes in Christ.'"2

The reality of growth without depth and many Christians being babes in Christ is very serious. One consequence is that people see no difference in Christians' lives compared with the lives of others. Many Christians have a negative witness in their lives. Dallas Willard writes about a well-known Christian leader who lost his faith, for so many of his mentors "stumbled and fell, never again to recover their faith."3 Finally the leader gave up his faith as well.

There are widely available discipleship programs and models offered by denominations and parachurch agencies, but a one-size-fits-all approach seldom works. Christian Schwarz states, "Countless church leaders around the globe have been inspired by the ministry of Willow Creek and have sought to build similar churches in their own contexts...They are in danger of missing the very secret that has made Willow Creek so successful...Do you really want to learn from Willow Creek? Then learn that they never imitated the model of another church."4

In 2004 Willow Creek itself asked, "Where are we?" and church leaders spent three years digesting research and analysis based on 2.6 million data points from more than eleven thousand completed surveys. Their research includes data from six other churches in addition to Willow Creek.5 They compiled the results in a book titled, *Reveal: Where Are You?* The authors discuss two segments of Christians at Willow Creek whose spiritual journeys are off track or who are experiencing dissatisfaction. The authors state, "But at the heart of their unhappiness may be the fact that neither segment seems to realize that much of the responsibility for their spiritual growth belongs to them. And it begs the question: Who should have pointed this out to them? Who should have helped them to begin taking more responsibility for their own spiritual growth?"6 It is this critical situation—common to churches all around the world—that this book seeks to address. The strategy described in this book is called "Micro-Macro Discipling," a simple, focused, and deep way to help Christians to get back on track in their spiritual growth journeys.

What Is Micro-Macro Discipling?

Micro-Macro Discipling is a theory and strategy that returns to the basics of a personal, intimate relationship with Jesus. It is the missing DNA in discipleship development. The micro level has as its foundation Acts 6:4, in which the biblical author stresses the importance of prayer and the Word. The theory is also a way toward Christlikeness. The micro-macro level is rooted in the parables of the sower and the growing seed: micro level as the very first stage—the stalk—which, if cared for properly, will eventually produce a great harvest, a macro level.

A Missing DNA in Discipleship Development

The reasons for this serious decline of Christianity are complex, but through my interviews with important Christian leaders (including their answers to question-naires), I have discovered that a missing element of DNA in the development of discipleship is the micro level of Micro-Macro Discipling.

The apostles of Jesus Christ in the early Church discovered this missing element when their ministry was being distracted. The apostles determined, "But we will devote ourselves to prayer, and to the ministry of the word" (Acts 6:4).[7] Neil Cole describes this as "the essential ministry of spreading God's word among the growing disciples."[8] Unfortunately, today's Western Church has allowed itself to be distracted from this vital ministry.

It is time for Christian leaders in the Western Church to make the same determination that these apostles made. It is not that Christian leaders need to lock themselves up for long amounts of time preparing for their sermons. But these leaders should commit to being fed by a steady and voluminous intake of Scripture with no purpose other than to hear from God and obey his voice. This should be an essential first step to any other strategy of discipleship.

Acts 6:4 – Prayer and the Word

When I was about to be consecrated a bishop in September 2009, I prayed fervently to our Lord Jesus Christ four months, asking what he wanted from me in this new role. The answer was exactly what Neil Cole said and what was in Acts 6:4. I deeply believe that the two key words, "prayer" and "Word," are the foundation for recap-turing the essence and energy of the early Church movement. I consider the meaning of the Word as the teaching of the Scriptures as well as the living Word of Christ himself that we must be attentive to him as he speaks through the Scriptures. Since then I have focused on these missing elements of DNA, and on influencing those people whom the Lord has entrusted me to oversee in regards to prayer and the Word. Through a focus on prayer and the Word, transformation has been hap-pening in those individuals' lives to glorify God through Micro-Macro Discipling.

A Way towards Christlikeness

John Stott, who is one of my spiritual fathers since 1992, asked me to bring our elder son Ignatius to see him in his home, St. Banarbas's House in London, in July 2009. He told us one thing that could change our lives. He said, "The most important word in my life is Christlikeness." In his book, *The Radical Disciple*, Stott writes, "God wants his people to become like Christ, for Christlikeness is the will of God for the people of God."[9] Christlikeness is not possible without a deep, constant connection to Jesus every day. I have named this connection, "Micro-Macro Discipling."

Mark 4: 28-29 – Jesus' Parable of the Growing Seed

In this direction, Micro-Macro Discipling is a mentoring discipleship strategy towards Christlikeness based firstly on the first stage of the parable of the growing seed in Mark 4: 28-29. Mark writes, "All by itself the soil produces grain – first the stalk, then the head, then the full kernel in the head. As soon as the grain is ripe, he puts the sickle to it, because the harvest has come." The missing DNA is the first stage – the stalk. And it is daily devotion – a daily intimate and personal relationship with God through prayers and reading the Bible. It is relational. It is missional. It is all about a lifestyle of Christlikeness. It is on a micro level that macro development of discipleship and kingdom growth can happen. Cole writes, "The growth of the Kingdom of God must start at the smallest of levels. A church is a complex entity with multiple cells. We must go further down microscopically, to the smallest unit of Kingdom life if we want to start the multiplication process."[10]

A Mentoring Discipleship Strategy

The purpose of this book is to present a mentoring discipleship strategy to develop a relational and missional lifestyle towards Christlikeness on a micro-macro level for those who want their lives to work. These three terms should be explained: "relational," "missional," and "micro-macro level." The "relational" aspect refers to the relationships between disciplers/mentors and disciples/mentorees. The "missional" aspect refers to leading people to Jesus and a broader sense in missional outreach and ministries. Finally, "micro-macro level" refers to the four levels of discipleship development according to Jesus' parable of the growing seed, starting with the first and basic steps in Christian formation, such as daily devotions and other basic Christian disciplines.

The Three Main Parts

This book contains three major sections. An effective strategy for kingdom development through a mentoring discipleship plan from the micro to the macro level must take into account the uniqueness of the context in which it will be implemented, so the first section of this book will address issues in this aspect. This first section explores the present crisis, especially the fact that fewer than 10 percent of Christians have a daily devotional time, which is directly related to the rationale for focusing on Micro-Macro Discipling.

I have travelled to various countries during the past seven years for the purpose of getting significant data for this book, including England, Rwanda, United States, Canada, and Hong Kong. I have interviewed quite a number of important Christian leaders, including John Stott, John Drane, Richard Peace, Terry Walling, Nicky Gumble, Gil Stieglitz, as well as three Anglican primates: Archbishop Yong Ping Chung, Archbishop Moses Tay, and Archbishop Emmanuel Kolini, and a number of Anglican bishops and clergy. All of them agree that the lack of daily devotion is perhaps the biggest problem for the universal Church, and most of them agree that the percentage of Christians committed to a daily time of devotion is less than 10 percent. They also agree that there are too few people trying to solve this problem.

The second section describes the biblical, ecclesiological, and theological assumptions that serve as the foundation of the strategy. This section attempts to clarify the goal of the process by asking three simple but basic questions: Why are fewer than 10 percent of Christians having a daily devotional time? Is this a problem? If so, how do we deal with this problem? A theology of Micro-Macro Discipling will be proposed, highlighting biblical teachings regarding the necessity and nature of this strategy.

The third section provides a practical mentoring discipleship plan to build up and live out a relational and missional lifestyle on a micro-macro level.[11] The section begins by outlining the tasks of a four-stage, simple, and gradual mentoring discipleship process. The final chapter will describe the effectiveness of this strategy after a five-year period.

---

[1] John Stott, *The Radical Disciple* (Downers Grove, IL: InterVarsity Press, 2010), 38.

[2] Greg Ogden, *Transforming Discipleship* (Downers Grove, IL: InterVarsity Press, 2003), 22.

[3] Dallas Willard, *The Divine Conspiracy* (New York: Harper One, 1997), 39-40.

[4] Christian A. Schwarz, *Color Your World with Natural Church Development* (St. Charles, IL: Church Smart Resources, 2005).

[5] Greg L. Hawkins and Cally Parkinson, *Reveal: Where Are You?* (Barrington, IL: Willow Creek Resources, 2007), 19.

[6] Ibid., 54.

[7] All biblical references are taken from the *New Revised Standard Version* unless otherwise noted.

[8] Neil Cole, *Cultivating a Life for God* (St. Charles, IL: Church Smart, 1999), 75.

[9] Stott, *The Radical Disciple*, 29.

[10] Cole, *Organic Church*, 98.

[11] The idea of a "micro-macro level" comes from Jesus' parable of the growing seeds in Mark 4:28. If the micro stage (i.e., the "stalk") works, then a macro effect ("harvest") will follow, and there will be thirty, sixty, or even a hundredfold. Mathematically, one hundredfold is 1,000,000,000,000, 000,000,000,000,000,000 (thirty zeros after 1). These four stages (from the micro- to the macro-level) involve raising up four kinds of leaders: disciplers, evangelists, mentors, and church planters.

PART ONE

CHAPTER ONE

THE PRESENT CRISIS

The church's ministry must be modeled after that of Jesus himself.
—*Eddie Gibbs, Church Next*

Don't plan on taking a vote on whether your church will release members to become
missionaries. What you must do is two things: create a culture informed by
missiology and create venues where people can practice being missionaries.
—*Reggie McNeal, The Present Future*

Taking into consideration the quotes above, particularly McNeal exhortation to "create venues where people can practice being missionaries," and Gibbs's encouragement that all missional efforts "must be modeled after the ministry of Jesus himself," it is clear that many churches do not have those venues and practices in place. This, in turn, makes it difficult for people to become true missionaries who follow Jesus model.

Quite a number of church leaders have focused on survival rather than growth. And there does not seem to be much growth, especially in North America and Europe. Why is this the case?

RESULTS OF A QUESTIONNAIRE ON DAILY DEVOTION

Megachurch Results

In November 2009, I was invited to teach a Master of Ministry course in a megachurch which has Sunday attendance numbers of about 5,000. I used that opportunity to test my theory of Micro-Macro Discipleship. I designed a simple questionnaire (see Appendix A) and asked the twenty-five students in the class to give the questionnaire to their small group members. A month later they provided me with the results of 323 completed questionnaires, which revealed that only 4.6 percent of the people in their small groups practice a daily devotional time (see Appendix B).

I asked the senior pastor a question that I have asked important Christian leaders all around the world. The question is, "What do you think is the percentage of Christians practicing a daily devotional time around the world?" His answer was, "Fewer than 10 percent," which is the same answer given by about 90 percent of the leaders I have asked. Then I asked him, "What do you think is the percentage of those in your church who are practicing a daily devotional time?" He answered, "I think we have been doing spiritual formation quite well. I think it would be approximately 40 to 50%."

A day later, when I preached in his church for the three Saturday services with a total attendance about two thousand people, I asked, "For those of you who have practiced a daily devotional time in the past twelve months, please raise your hands." The pastor nearly fainted every time I asked this question, for in all three services there were fewer than 3 percent of the people raising their hands. This was shocking to me, since his church is one of the few fast-growing and solid churches. The next week when he preached at all six services, he asked his people to repent for not practicing a daily time of intimate relationship with God, and he told them that the whole church should endeavor to improve on this devastating spiritual dryness.

The questionnaire especially designed for the Master of Ministry course at the megachurch was to test whether a Christian was enjoying a daily intimate relationship with God. It was a test to show whether someone is living a relational and missional lifestyle and whether the individual is experiencing the fruit of a Christlike lifestyle. Based upon the results of the questionnaire from the megachurch (see Appendix B), it is clear that two things naturally happen when people practice a daily devotional time several times a week.

First, the more relational someone is with God through daily devotion, the more the individual experienced abundance (that is, a daily experience of wellness in one's life). Similarly, the more relational someone is with God through daily devotion, the more missional he or she became by bringing more relatives and friends to church. This questionnaire is simple, focused, and deep in a way that shows the devastating state of the Church when it is missing the personal daily relationship with Jesus through practices of prayer and study of the Word.

Smaller Church Results

After receiving the results from that megachurch, I designed a revised questionnaire (Appendix C) because I realized that even Christians who have a daily devotional time might be doing so for the wrong purposes. They might have a daily devotional time out of guilt or out of a sense that they would be punished by God or looked down upon by their pastors and other leaders if they did not do so. Or they might have a daily devotional time because of a sense of duty, especially if the individual is a leader. In these situations, the individual will not achieve an intimate, personal relationship with God.

Another erroneous way to approach one's devotional time is to see it as an opportunity to study the Word of God. In dealing with this kind of mentality, Cole has an important point: "What is really lacking? Knowledge is not lacking; obedience is. Christians in America are already educated beyond their obedience, and more education is not the solution.[1] For people who have a daily devotional time solely for the purpose of study, this does not necessarily bring them into a daily intimate personal relationship with God. On the other hand, if those Christians enjoy their daily devotional times because of an intimate personal relationship with God, then at the same time it can also be a good way to learn more about the Word of God.

In June 2010, the updated questionnaires were sent to all fifteen churches under my jurisdiction as a bishop. Eleven churches completed the questionnaire, comprising a total of 438 people. This number is fewer than 50 percent of all those in the fifteen churches. The results indicate that after one year of intense encouragement and teaching of the importance of daily devotion, only 18 percent have daily devotions seven days a week (Appendix D). The results also show that 46 percent of people have zero to three days of devotion, and 54 percent of people have four to seven days of devotion.

On the abundance and missional side, the results are similar in each setting. The more devotional time one has, the more one experiences wellness on a daily basis, and the more often one brings relatives and friends to church. One negative result is that there are not many people from the fifteen churches under my oversight who are bringing new friends to church. When "relational" and "missional" do not go together, this is a sign that there may be quite a number of people who do not have connections with non-believers or who do not want to have connections with non-believers.

CHALLENGES

Relationship with God and Each Other

John Drane writes, "A more discerning question will be not, 'How many of us are there?' but 'How much like Christ have we become?' – remembering that Jesus himself left only eleven key disciples to change the world."[2] Our challenge is not to increase in numbers but rather to build a momentum to be more relational with God and with each other. As Drane states, this is a challenge to have a lifestyle of Christlikeness. A significant part of growing in Christlikeness, according to the Micro-Macro Discipling theory, is first of all to practice daily devotion. Willard writes, "So the kingdom of the heavens, from the practical point of view in which we all must live, is simply our experience of Jesus' continual interaction with us in history and throughout the days, hours, and moments of our earthly existence."[3]

A daily intimate relationship with Jesus and the ability to hear what Jesus says to us through the Bible is the key to being a true disciple of Christ and the key to genuine Kingdom growth. Without taking this challenge seriously, it is not possible deal with other problems. Willard writes, "With assistance from those who understand the divine voice from their own experience and with an openness and will to learn on our part, we can come to recognize the voice of God without great difficulty."[4] This needs to take priority over all other ways to help people to be mature Christians so that the parable of the growing seed may happen to the lives of Christians and churches.

Raising Up Disciplers

Another challenge for Christians is to raise up disciplers. Willard contends that non-discipleship is "the elephant in the church":

> What can it mean to us now to make disciples with the disappearance of Jesus as teacher? You cannot have students if you have no teacher. Some time back, a drug rehabilitation program ran an interesting commercial that showed an elephant walking around in an ordinary home, going by the son doing homework, the wife washing dishes, and so forth. Everyone studiously tries to ignore it, but it is obviously the biggest thing around the house. Non-discipleship is the elephant in the church.[5]

One of the main reasons why most Christians do not know how to practice daily devotion is because they do not have disciplers to help them learn how to do so. Willard writes, "If we are to follow Jesus' directions and make students of him from all ethnic groups, or 'nations,' we must be his students, and we must intend to lead others to be his students."[6] It is for this reason that we need to raise up more disciplers and help Christians to be aware of the importance of discipleship.

Growth in Being Missional

We also need to take up the challenge to become more missional. Gibbs explains the meaning of the term "missional" as it relates to the Christian Church:

> What is a "missional church"? The term missional, which we are using in relation to churches in North America and other parts of the Western world, draws attention to the essential nature and vocation of the church as God's called and sent people. It sees the church primarily as the instrument of God's mission. Following Lesslie Newbigin and others, a church that is missional understands that God's mission calls and sends the church of Jesus Christ, to be a missionary church in its own society and in the cultures in which it finds itself.[7]

In order to become missional, churches must raise up apostles. Martin Garner points out that nothing is more important than raising, sending, and releasing apostles. He writes, "Most [church] programmes, structures and expressions add value to the church, but they are a second stage. The first stage in pioneering mission is not a program, a structure, or a plan but a person – a person called an apostle."[8] He continues, "We need a fresh 'sending out' and 'releasing' of apostles so that they may do the work God has called them to do."[9] In the minds of traditional Christians, "apostles" are the bishops. But apostolic ministry is about more than simply having bishops. The Church today needs more apostles to lead the churches to be more missional so that there are more disciplers, evangelists, mentors, and church planters. Gibbs writes that "the "baton" of the Great Commission mandate – to disciple all peoples of the world – has to be passed from one generation of discipling apostles to the next."[10]

Recent Strategy for Developing Discipleship

Neil Cole writes, "God has already given us all we need. All we have to do is look at simple things once again, in another light."[11] To make this Micro-Macro Discipling movement a success and to bring about change, transformation, and momentum, two areas will be at the core: prayer and the Word.

After more than a year of interviews, compiling data based upon the questionnaires, and three face-to-face consultations with theology professors (Eddie Gibbs in Pasadena, California, Gil Stieglitz in Sacramento, California, and Terry Walling in Chico, California), I wrote a four-year plan for the fifteen churches that I oversee as bishop.

I then invited Professor Terry Walling, from Fuller Theological Seminary's Doctor of Ministry program, to Seattle for a three-day retreat with our Network Leadership Team, comprised of five clergy, myself included. We discussed the proposal and produced a document. On October 29, 2010, delegates of our Annual General Meeting passed this document unanimously (see Appendix E). We believe that this concise and innovative strategic plan based on the principle of Micro-Macro Discipling and Jesus' parable of the growing seed will bring us into a new paradigm of Kingdom growth. In the mandate of my apostolic ministry, prayer and the Word are the reason, centre, and focus of our lifestyle of Christlikeness. A great deal of hard work has been done to help our members to understand, experience, practice, and enjoy this essential lifestyle as disciples of Christ.

PRAYER

Prayer and daily devotion seem to be the two most forgotten ways that most Christians are practicing their faith. Ed Silvoso writes, "Israel's only weapon was prayer. No army, no economic power, no social status. Nothing. What set them free and gave them victory over Pharaoh's mighty army? Prayer. Likewise, the Early Church's only weapon was prayer (Acts 1:14; 2:42; 4:24-31). We are called to do the same, beginning with our own Jerusalem. Prayer is the key to successfully accomplish it."[12] Prayer is of utmost importance. In light of this I have launched two major campaigns: the twenty-four hour prayer campaign and the annual 40-day fast during Lent. In addition to these new initiatives, prayer and fasting is encouraged on many levels.

Twenty-four Hour Prayer Campaign for 1,100 Days

A twenty-four-hour prayer campaign has been launched since August 2009 through my first online blog.[13] This is one of the methods to teach and encourage people to know the importance and power of prayer. For 1,100 days, people primarily from our churches have been praying for our leaders, members, and ministries. Each of the one hundred participants logged on to the blog and signed up for the hours that they would pray.

Encouragement of Prayer on All Levels

Our leaders have encouraged all members to pray at many different times, both individually and corporately. Some of the ways that have been suggested include: personal daily devotions, increased times of prayer in small groups, higher participation in the weekly prayer meetings, commitment to participating in the twenty-four hour prayer campaign, commitment to the prayer ministry team, and participation in many fasting campaigns, including two 100-day fasts, one 3-day fast called "Operation Esther," and an annual 40-day fast during in Lent. Moreover, in 2016, we started a whole-year 366 days morning prayer from 6:30 a.m. to 7:30 a.m. Monday through Friday, 8 a.m. to 9:30 a.m. on Saturday, and 7:30 a.m. to 8:30 a.m. on Sunday.

THE WORD

The ministry of the Word is the essence of the parable of the growing seed and the key to discipleship development. I have made two major contributions in this regard. The first includes three blogs and podcasts – "Devotion on Fire," "Discipler 123," and "Break.Build" – which are daily devotion blogs. The "Devotion on Fire" blog consists of a three-year and three-month daily devotion to go through the whole Bible, one chapter a day. "Discipler 123" consists of a daily devotion with commentary through the whole Bible. "Break.Build" is a forty-day daily devotion based on Jesus' Sermon on the Mount, tailor-made to those who have not started daily devotion or to use as a forty-day spiritual journey with Jesus during Lent. My second contribution is the launch of the "Discipler 123" campaign, teaching and encouraging Christians to be disciplers by meeting with new Christians for three months in a one-on-one or one-on-two setting. Both of these aim to build momentum toward study of the Word and, ultimately, discipleship development. At the time of this writing, people from 114 countries are currently visiting or have visited those blogs/podcast, with more than a million total visits.

"Devotion on Fire," "Discipler 123," and "Break.Build"
Daily Devotion Blogs/Podcast

Gibbs discusses the unfortunate phenomenon of the "optional" devotional time in his book, *ChurchNext*. He writes,

> Traditionally, evangelicals have placed great emphasis on the importance of sustaining a daily "quiet time" as an essential discipline in maintaining one's walk with God and of growing in the Christian life. Many individuals could not maintain the daily discipline, while others reacted against a perceived legalism and opted to read the Bible as and when the Spirit moved them. One would hope that they would have read it with greater, not less, frequency than prevailed when they were driven by "legalism."[14]

In order to lead this Micro-Macro Discipling movement and set a good example personally, I have been writing a daily blog since July 2009. First was the "Devotion on Fire" blog, which began in July 2009 and was completed in November 2012. And second was the "Discipler 123" blog/podcast, which started in March 2011 and continues presently. Then third was the "Break.Build" blog/podcast, which started in February 2014. In these three blogs I encourage using the essence of *lectio divina* so that Christians have a helpful devotional method. Gibbs describes this Bible-reading discipline: "The practice of *lection divina* (literally, 'divine reading,' signifying meditation on Scripture) is especially appropriate for Boomers and Gen Xers who have already experimented with various non-Christian meditation techniques for looking inward to find divine light."[15]

There have been more than one million visits to the three blogs since they began, and hundreds of Christians, including bishops and leaders from 114 countries, have been using the blogs as their way of having daily devotions. I have received hundreds of appreciation emails, letters, or cards expressing how people are being helped and mentored through the blogs (see Appendix F). There are three reasons for people to use the blogs as daily devotion: for a healthy spiritual diet, as a good example of spiritual journaling, and as an online discipler.

First, the "Discipler 123" blog can be used to help a believer maintain a healthy spiritual diet. On the blog I encourage people to read one chapter of the Bible daily. As John Stott writes, "Just as the secret of the healthy growth of a child is the regularity of a right diet, so daily disciplined feeding is the major condition of spiritual growth."[16] John Drane exhorts believers to read even more of the Bible daily: "Why do we mostly read the Bible only in short sections, when we say it is the most important book in the world?"[17] Reading one chapter of the Bible a day should be the minimum; to read any less would render a believer spiritually starving.

Reading one chapter of the Bible each day is a habit that every Christian should be able to develop. In their book, *Connecting: The Mentoring Relationships You Need to Succeed in Life*, Paul Stanley and Robert Clinton point out why most Christians do not have this habit:

> In order to know and follow Christ, a disciple needs to establish habits that will affect his or her character and destiny. Such habits are essential to the disciple's lifelong pursuit of Christ. Habits do not develop easily; human nature resists change. Steven Covey, in his book, *The Seven Habits of Highly Effective People*, compares the effort needed to break or establish habits to the great amount of energy initially needed by a rocket to overcome the earth's gravitational pull. Once out of the earth's atmosphere, however, the rocket glides with small amounts of energy.[18]

The blog also provides an example of spiritual journaling. Since the Bible has 1,189 chapters, I have committed to keep this blog for 1,189 days and to use it as my personal, daily spiritual journal. I write down what I hear from Jesus and how I experience his intimate relationship with me each day. It is my hope that my journal will encourage more Christians to write their own spiritual journals.

A third use of the blog is as an online discipler. One of the reasons that so many Christians do not have daily devotions is because they do not have disciplers to show them how. The best way for a new believer to become a mature Christian is to have a discipler walk with him or her for a certain period of time so that daily devotions become a good habit. It is also helpful for a new believer to be part of a small group of two to three people in which the members encourage and are accountable to each other in regards to their daily devotions. I offer myself as a daily online discipler to walk with those who use my blog to enrich their spiritual journeys.

"Discipler 123" Campaign

The first year of my four-year plan includes raising up disciplers. Stanley and Clinton provide the following description of a discipler: "A discipler-mentor teaches and enables a mentoree in the basics of following Christ."[19] Everyone from our churches received an invitation to be a discipler. They received an introductory leaflet, a pen with the phrase, "Discipler 123," and the website of my blog (http://discipler123.blogspot. com) to create momentum for this campaign. This campaign was launched on March 1, 2011 and continued for three months. It is hoped that those who commit to being disciplers will disciple their mentorees for one to three years. In his book, *Transforming Discipleship*, Ogden writes,

> Jesus is saying that discipleship training is not about information transfer, from head to head, but imitation, life to life...Disciple making is about relational investment. It is walking alongside a few invited fellow travelers in an intentional relationship over time. You will hear this constant refrain: Disciple making is not a program but a relationship...If we are to follow the model of Jesus, apprenticeship should be a part of all that we do so that ministry can be multiplied."[20]

We follow the format for discipleship that is presented by Ogden in *Transforming Discipleship*. Ogden proposes the following:

> Three people journey together for a year to a year and a half while they grow toward maturity and being equipped to disciple others. As this relationship comes to a close, the challenge comes to each person to invite two others into the same walk of faith and then reproduce, and so on. Over the five-to seven-year period of multiplying discipleship triads, it is common to have eighty to a hundred or more people who have been carefully groomed in the context of an intimate relationship. This number of self-initiating, reproducing disciples has a tremendous impact

on the climate of a ministry. It takes only 10 to 20 percent of a congregation to set the tone for the whole. Invest in those who will set the pace for the rest.[21]

I am a leader who leads by example. I started with many others to participate in the Discipler 123 Campaign. I discipled two young men for two and a half years. One was my thirteen-year-old son Athanasius and the other was his best friend Vance, who is my godson. I taught them about daily devotion and I practiced daily devotions with them between January 2009 and May 2011. I hope to set a good example to the people in our churches that offering oneself to be a discipler has great benefit. Both of them have become vibrant and anointed youth leaders today.

---

[1] Cole, *Organic Church*, 151.

[2] John Drane, *The McDonaldization of the Church: Spirituality, Creativity and the Future of the Church* (London: Darton, Longman & Todd, 2000), 41.

[3] Willard, *The Divine Conspiracy*, 280.

[4] Dallas Willard, *Hearing God* (Downers Grove, IL: InterVarsity Press, 1999), 169.

[5] Willard, *The Divine Conspiracy*, 301.

[6] Ibid., 305.

[7] Eddie Gibbs, *ChurchNext: Quantum Changes in How We Do Ministry* (Downers Grove, IL: InterVarsity Press, 2000), 51.

[8] Martin Garner, *A Call for Apostles Today* (Cambridge, UK: Grove Books, 2007), 3.

[9] Ibid., 23.

[10] Gibbs, *ChurchNext*, 222.

[11] Cole, *Organic Church*, xxix.

[12] Ed Silvoso, *That None Should Perish* (Ventura, CA: Regal, 1995), 192.

[13] "Bishop Silas" blog, http://bishopsilas.blogspot.com (accessed July 2009). This is my personal blog.

[14] Gibbs, *ChurchNext*, 133.

[15] Ibid., 135.

[16] Stott, *The Radical Disciple*, 87.

[17] Drane, *The McDonaldization of the Church*, 71.

[18] Paul Stanley and Robert Clinton, *Connecting: The Mentoring Relationships You Need to Succeed in Life* (Colorado Springs: NavPress, 1992), 52. Stanley and Clinton reference Steven Covey's book, *The Seven Habits of Highly Effective People* (New York: Free Press, 1989), 46-47.

[19] Stanley and Clinton, *Connecting*, 51.

[20] Ogden, *Transforming Discipleship*, 86, 17, and 91.

[21] Ibid., 128-29.

CHAPTER TWO

REESEARCH ON THE PRESENT GENERAL PRACTICE OF DAILY DEVOTION

This chapter recounts several personal interviews related to the percentage of Christians having daily devotion. The interviewees included the following important Christian leaders: Rev. Dr. John Drane (completed February 2009), Rev. Dr. Gil Stieglitz (completed April 2009), Rev. Dr. John Stott (completed July 2009), and Archbishop Yong Ping Chung (completed September 2009), among others. In addition, this chapter conveys the information I gleaned while teaching a Master of Ministry course, "Micro-Macro Discipling," at a Bible Institute of a 5,000-member megachurch to test the Micro-Macro Discipling theory (completed November 2009). Finally, this chapter will consider the results of a questionnaire completed by 1,179 Christians in forty-six churches. Special attention will be given to the implications of those results.

It is important to note that whether or not one has daily devotions is not the only means by which to measure discipleship. However, one's daily devotional time is a vital sign of a relationship with Jesus Christ, and after many interviews and statistical findings, the devastating reality is that the daily devotional time has been neglected. The Church needs disciplers who will help other Christians to have an intimate relationship with Jesus Christ through daily devotions and other basic Christian disciplines. In fact, from the results of my wide-spectrum research, fewer than 10 percent of Christians have a daily devotional time. Out of that 10 percent, many have a daily devotional time because of guilt, duty, or study, and are not able to establish a personal and intimate relationship with Jesus.

Results of Interviews with Significant Christian Leaders

Several Christian leaders were interviewed as part of the research base for this study. These include: Rev. Dr. John Stott, Rev. Dr. John Drane, Rev. Dr. Gil Steiglitz, Rev. Dr. Richard Peace, Rev. Dr. Rick Warren, Archbishop Ping Chung Yong, Rev. Dr. Terry Walling, Rev. Peter Ho, and several Rwandan bishops with the Anglican Church of Rwanda. Each interview has contributed to an understanding of the pulse of the Church in terms of daily devotion.

Rev. Dr. John Stott

"Uncle John" had been one of my spiritual fathers since 1991. John passed away on July 27, 2011. My son Ignatius and I were so blessed that he welcomed us to his home in England on July 18, 2009. During this visit, I told John that when I prayed to the Lord Jesus Christ regarding what he wanted me to do when I became a bishop, Jesus' answer was, "Do what is in Acts 6: 4, 'We will give our attention to prayer and the ministry of the Word." I then shared with him the Micro-Macro Discipling vision and how the Lord told me to help our people to establish an intimate relationship with him through prayer and to teach them to listen to Jesus' Word.

When John heard this he smiled, looked at me with the loving eyes of a father, and said, "Silas, you are right on. Yes, I believe so. Let me give you what I heard from the Lord to you." Then he asked Ignatius to read 1 Thessalonians 2:1-13:

> You yourselves know, brothers and sisters, that our coming to you was not in vain, but though we had already suffered and been shamefully mistreated at Philippi, as you know, we had courage in our God to declare to you the gospel of God in spite of great opposition. For our appeal does not spring from deceit or impure motives or trickery, but just as we have been approved by God to be entrusted with the message of the gospel, even so we speak, not to please mortals, but to please God who tests our hearts. As you know and as God is our witness, we never came with words of flattery or with a pretext for greed; nor did we seek praise from mortals, whether from you or from others, though we might have made demands as apostles of Christ. But we were gentle among you, like a nurse tenderly caring for her own children. So deeply do we care for you that we are determined to share with you not only the gospel of God but also our own selves, because you have become very dear to us.

> You remember our labor and toil, brothers and sisters; we worked night and day, so that we might not burden any of you while we

proclaimed to you the gospel of God. You are witnesses, and God also, how pure, upright, and blameless our conduct was toward you believers. As you know, we dealt with each one of you like a father with his children, urging and encouraging you and pleading that you lead a life worthy of God, who calls you into his own kingdom and glory.

We also constantly give thanks to God for this, that when you received the word of God that you heard from us, you accepted it not as a human word but as what it really is, God's word, which is also at work in you believers.

John told me that this is what he heard from the Lord for me. He told Ignatius to stop three times – when he read the words "mother," "father," and "word. He explained that these were the three key words he had received from the Lord Jesus Christ for me in two aspects: first, to have the gentleness of a mother and the passion of a father to build up relationship between God and his people, and second, to be a steward of God's Word.

John confirmed the findings of my research. First, he said, it is true that fewer than 10 percent of Christians practice daily devotion. This reality makes it impossible for the Parable of the Growing Seed to take place, as the growth must take place from "stalk, head, full kernel, to harvest." Without a daily intimate personal relationship with Jesus, the stage stops at the first phase – the stalk -- or it may even wither at this stage. Second, John explained that every Christian needs a good discipler to help for a period of time (Jesus used three years) to ensure a healthy daily devotion habit. As Stanley and Clinton clearly state in *Connecting*,

In order to know and follow Christ, a disciple needs to establish habits that will affect his or her character and destiny. Such habits are essential to the disciple's lifelong pursuit of Christ. Habits do not develop easily; human nature resists change...The effort needed to break or establish habits to the great amount of energy initially needed by a rocket to overcome the earth's gravitational pull. Once out of the earth's atmosphere, however, the rocket glides with small amounts of energy.[1]

John then gave me his new book, which he wrote in 2006, titled, *Through the Bible through the Year*. I was surprised to receive his gift because the Lord's idea for me do a "1,189 days of Daily Devotion" through my blog was similar to the idea that John had in this new book. He went through the whole Bible in a year in a daily devotional format for the reader. I told John about my vision and he smiled again and told me that it was a very good and accurate vision from the Lord.

During this time with John, I was encouraged by the fact that John had heard from the Lord on my behalf, and that much of what he had heard from the Lord was a confirmation of what I had heard from the Lord in May 2009. I was blessed by this miracle of receiving such confirmation and blessings from the Lord through John Stott.

Rev. Dr. John Drane

John Drane is a professor in Fuller's Doctor of Ministry program. I took his course, "New Ways of Being Church," in February 2008 in England. In February 2009, I conversed with him via email, and asked him what he thought was the percentage of Christians having daily devotion, and how critical the question was. His reply is as follows:

> What you say about daily devotions absolutely connects with our experience. In fact, I am surprised it is as high as 10%, and my suspicion would be that if you were to inquire further as to what "daily devotions" amounts to for even that small number, you would likely discover that it doesn't occupy much time in a typical day. From what I can see, I would say that this is a much bigger problem for Christians from evangelical type backgrounds that don't have (or want) a liturgical tradition: at least with the Daily Office, you have a fixed body of material that takes up a specific amount of time, whereas if you are in effect inventing it yourself each day (or even using things like Bible reading plans) it doesn't seem to engender the same level of either habit or commitment.

> Mentoring – absolutely, you are right, and I think this is connected to the question of daily devotions. Because part of the reason so few Christians engage in traditional devotions is that their lifestyles have changed in terms of the times they need to be in work, the

demands of family life, etc., so in a way I wouldn't personally want to be too critical of those who say they have no devotions, because I think we should be asking a more fundamental question, about what such devotion might now look like in the light of changed circumstances. And mentoring will definitely play a part in that. But, I suspect, not mentoring so that they go back to the patterns of previous generations, but mentoring that will journey alongside people and take account of where they actually find themselves, rather than where the church might wish them to be. Whatever "solving the problem" might look like, I think it is bound to look different from what was the norm in the past.

Drane confirmed the finding in my research that there are far fewer than 10 percent of Christians who are having daily devotion. He adds that there is likely a bigger problem for Christians from evangelical churches than from liturgical churches because of the daily office tradition of liturgical traditions. It is likely more difficult for Christians from evangelical churches to form a habit or commitment. Drane also confirmed that the lack of devotion for 90 percent of Christians is due to the fact that they do not have mentors to help them to develop this kind of basic relationship with Jesus.

Rev. Dr. Gil Stieglitz

Dr. Steiglitz has been my personal coach since 2005, helping me to have a deeper level of leadership development. He agrees with my Micro Discipleship theory and agrees that the situation of fewer than 10 percent of Christians having daily devotion is a huge problem that most Christian leaders are not addressing. He supports me fully in terms of the further development of this Micro Discipleship strategy, and he has encouraged me to take it to a wider spectrum of churches so that more churches and Christians might benefit.

Rev. Dr. Richard Peace

In May 2009 I took Dr. Peace's final project symposium at Fuller Theological Seminary. During this course, I met with him and asked the two questions regarding his prediction of the percentage of Christians having daily devotions, as well as the importance of this. In response, Dr. Peace agreed that the number is likely fewer than 10 percent. He added that the situation is "a big deal indeed."

Rev. Dr. Rick Warren

Pastor Rick Warren preached at my consecration as a bishop on September 9, 2009 in Pasadena, California. I then interviewed him in May 2011 at the Exponential conference in Orlando, Florida. Rev. Warren agreed that agreed that the number is likely fewer than 10 percent. In response to whether this is significant, he replied, "Yes, this is the biggest problem in the church right now and it seems nobody knows. That is why I have been writing a daily devotion blog for quite some years."

Archbishop Yong Ping Chung

Archbishop Yong has been one of my spiritual fathers since 2004. He agreed that my finding of fewer than 10 percent of Christians having daily devotion is the biggest relational problem for Christians worldwide. When he was the bishop of the Anglican Church of Sabah, he initiated a movement called "Disciple 113." This movement was to raise up one discipler to help one non-Christian to receive Christ, and then to follow that new convert for three years. This movement was a great success in the 1980s. It helped to increase the total number of Anglicans in Sabah after six years from nine thousand to seventeen thousand. Archbishop Yong was one of the main speakers at our National Conference this past year. He has helped me to put the Micro Discipleship plan into practice, and will be continuing to help me in the same role for the coming three years.

Rev. Dr. Terry Walling

Dr. Walling has been my personal coach since October 2010. He told me that by the launching of the Micro Discipleship strategy I have found a missing DNA for discipleship development which can help the Church, many pastors, Christian leaders, and Christians. He helped me to streamline the four-year plan for Micro Discipleship, which has been presented in Chapter 1 and which will be explained in further detail in Chapters 7 and 8. Dr. Walling has been one of the three main speakers at the ACiC National Conference for the past two years, and he will continue in the same role for the coming two years. He agrees that fewer than 10 percent of Christians are having daily devotion.

He has stated that this phenomenon causes great problems for the whole Church and yet nobody is aware of the destructive force of this situation.

Several Rwandan Bishops of the Anglican Church of Rwanda

Another source of research included several Rwandan bishops who are my colleagues in the Anglican Church of Rwanda. All of them surprisingly stated that they thought the percentage of Christians having daily devotion worldwide was under 5 percent or even under 1 percent. Those archbishops and bishops who thought the percentage was under 5 percent were Archbishop Emmanuel Kolini (retired Primate), Archbishop Onesphore Rwaje (current Primate), Bishop Augustin Ahimana, Bishop Nathan Gasatura, Bishop Jered Kalimba, Bishop Laurent Mbanda, Bishop Louis Muvunyi, Bishop Augustin Mvunabandi, and Bishop Geoffrey Rwubusisi. Those bishops who thought the percentage was under 1 percent were Bishop Josias Sendegeya and Bishop Alexis Bilindabagabo.

Questionnaire Completed at a 5,000-Member Megachurch

The questionnaire was initially given to the twenty-five Master of Ministry students who were leading small groups. As described in Chapter 1, a total of 383 questionnaires were returned. The result was that fewer than 5 percent of the small group members were having daily devotion. This particular questionnaire likely contains the most accurate data due to the fact that later questionnaire results may be skewed by the fact that some church members began to have daily devotions as a result of my efforts. But this original result reflects the seriousness of the situation (see Appendix B).

The results reveal three important findings. First, the percentage of those having devotion on all seven days was just 4.6 percent. Second, the more often one has daily devotion, the higher are the abundance levels for that individual. Third, those who have daily devotion more often are more likely to bring others to church.

Questionnaire Completed by 1,179 Christians from Forty-Six Churches

Since the first questionnaire was distributed at the megachurch four years ago, a few hundred pastors have been asked to distribute the same questionnaire to the members of their congregations. Unfortunately, fewer than 10 percent of those pastors returned the completed questionnaires, and most of them were only able to have about 10 percent of their members complete the questionnaire. In all, 1,179 questionnaires were received from forty-six churches (see Appendix D).

The results based upon these 1,179 completed questionnaires were that 16 percent of the believers are having daily devotions. It is also important to note that this percentage may be skewed by the fact that many of those completing the questionnaire may have only recently renewed their commitment to daily devotion. Similarly to the results from the megachurch, there was also a correspondence between more frequent daily devotions and a higher abundance level, as well as a correspondence between more frequent daily devotions and a proclivity to bringing others to church. Also, the questionnaire notes that there are quite a number of Christians having devotions out of guilt, duty, and study rather than to encourage their own intimate personal relationships with Jesus.

Summary

The interviews and questionnaires reveal a very clear deficit of discipleship development. Additionally, it is telling that most Christians I approached did not have the intention of completing the questionnaire. There may be several reasons for this: first, some may believe that devotion is not their concern and they simply did not want to bother with the questionnaire; second, others may not have wanted to face the reality of their lack of devotion; third, still others may not have wanted their senior pastors to know their lack of devotion; and fourth, some senior pastors may not have wanted me to know the reality of their churches.[2] If this micro stage of discipleship development is not developed, and if churches fail to recognize this, then more serious decline will take place within many denominations and churches in the coming ten years. My call is to sound the alarm and to suggest a simple, focused, and deep way to turn the "Titanic" around from a major disaster.

---

[1] Stanley and Clinton, *Connecting*, 52.

[2] Unfortunately, some senior pastors wanted their congregants to directly forward the results to me via email. The problem with this was that it is impossible to maintain anonymity when using email, and many likely did not want to reveal their names.

CHAPTER THREE

RATIONALE FOR LAUNCHING MICRO DISCIPLESHIP

When the foundations are being destroyed, what can the righteous do?
—Psalm 11:3

Some time ago I spoke with Dr. Terry Walling, a Fuller DMin program professor and my personal coach. The first thing he said was a shock to me. He said,

> Silas, you won't believe this. I had a coaching conference with two famous pastors yesterday and they both got into some kind of troubles. When I asked them to take another angle to look at things and to suggest to them that they needed sometime to be with Jesus, both of them did not know how to respond. Because both of them told me it was a long time since they had been with Jesus. I think your Micro-Macro Discipling is really a missing DNA for many pastors!

I was surprised to hear this because Dr. Walling told me some months ago that he thought the Micro-Macro Discipling strategy is a missing DNA to discipleship development, but now it is apparently a missing DNA for many pastors as well. It is difficult for people to believe that many pastors neglect their own relationship with Jesus. Perhaps that is one of the main reasons why so many churches are "on life support," according to Reggie McNeal.[1]

Recently, one of the two small groups I have been leading had a Thanksgiving dinner together. At least ten members of this group thanked me for my continuous persistency to urge them to have a real daily devotion, a truly daily intimate personal relationship with Jesus. These members have been using my two daily devotion blogs for their daily devotion. Some of them started in 2009 when I started to write my daily blog, "Devotion on Fire," to encourage Christians to have daily devotion, while others started in 2012 using my new blog/podcast "Discipler123," which added English and Chinese (Cantonese) podcasts. All of them confirmed that they experienced a change in their relationship with Jesus after using the blogs. They all tasted the sweetness of a daily intimate personal relationship with Jesus. The group leader, Lucy Ng, said, "Silas, if you did not challenge me to have daily devotion two years ago, I would have left the church because I did not feel my faith was real. Thank you for leading me back to Jesus!" Lucy is now one of our interns and has been at Regent College for the past three years preparing to be a pastor.

Robert Quinn, in his book, *Deep Change*, explains that "we must continually choose between deep change or slow death."[2] He writes that deep change is very different from what we usually call change, which is "incremental change as the result of a rational analysis and planning process...We feel we are in control."[3] On the other hand, "deep change effort distorts existing patterns of action and involves taking risks. Deep change means surrendering control...It is therefore natural for each of us to deny that there is any need for a deep change."[4]

Deep change is needed in today's western Church in order to avoid facing a slow death. Neil Cole discusses this, as well as what kinds of foundations have been destroyed, in his book, *Cultivating a Life for God*. He writes,

> Given this view of the expansion of the church and the power of God's word we can certainly understand why the apostles would conclude, "It is not desirable for us to neglect the word of God" (Acts 6:2). Instead of being distracted from the essential ministry of spreading God's word among the growing disciples, they determined, "But we will devote ourselves to prayer, and to the ministry of the word" (Acts 6:4).
>
> Unfortunately, today's Western church has allowed herself to be distracted from this vital ministry. It's time for Christian leaders in the Western church to make the same determination that these apostles made. Not that we need to lock ourselves up for even longer time in the study preparing for our sermons, but rather be fed by a steady and voluminous intake of Scripture with no purpose other than to hear from God and obey His voice![5]

The rationale for launching Micro-Macro Discipling is that Christians are heading for a slow death and desperately need a deep change. Ample examples reveal that many churches are on a slow death path. Jesus calls his followers to surrender control so that they can follow him. He says, "If anyone would come after me, he must deny himself and take up his cross and follow me" (Matthew 16:24). There are so many models of discipleship development to follow, but often believers miss the first level because they miss the teacher. As Dallas Willard states,

> We have no effective bridge from the faith to the life. Right at the heart of this alienation lies the absence of Jesus the teacher from our lives. Strangely, we seem prepared to learn how to live from almost anyone but him. We are ready to believe that the "latest studies" have more to teach us about love and sex than he does, and that Louis Rukeyser knows more about finances (page 55). . . .The disappearance of Jesus as teacher explains why today in Christian churches – of whatever leaning – little effort is made to teach people to do what he did and taught.[6]

This chapter analyzes the devastating situation of the absence of church growth and a critical numerical decline in many denominations. It focuses on the phenomenon in Canada of church "leavers," Christians without churches, and the abundance of transfer-growth in churches rather than salvation-growth.

Church Leavers

According to Dave and Jon Ferguson in their book, *Exponential*, every week 43,000 Christians in North America are leaving the Church for good.[7] Cole states that churches in America lose 2,765,000 people each year, and between 3,500 and 4,000 churches close their doors each year for the last time, while only 1100-1500 churches are started. Not a single county in all America has a greater percentage of churched people today than a decade ago.[8]

In the past, people joining churches or leaving churches was a general phenomenon. There has historically been little research related to the reasons why people leave churches. Alan Jamieson's books, *A Churchless Faith* and *Church Leavers*, present surprising data regarding a new phenomenon related to church leavers.[9] Jamieson found that many of those leavers were core leaders of their churches and their leaving seemed odd. He repeats a comment made by a businessman who could not understand why churches did not do anything about this phenomenon of leaders leaving: "That would never happen in the corporate world because that information [that the leaders have] is like gold."[10] Indeed, church leaders should look more carefully at "backdoor leavers." According to Jamieson's finding, there are several reasons for the rising trend of church leavers. These reasons include loneliness, dysfunction of church structures and leaders, the feeling that "It doesn't work for me," lack of community, lack of discipleship models, and what John Drane refers to as a "fast-food mentality" regarding church.

The first issue is loneliness. Jamieson quotes one church leader as saying, "I found that I really had no peers in the church...I didn't have a friend or a close soul-mate who I felt was going the same place as me."[11] The loneliness in this church leader's life reflects a real situation that is occurring in many churches today. Leaders have ministries, but many are without close relationships or friends.

The second issue is dysfunctional churches and dysfunctional leaders. Jamieson states clearly that dysfunction related to church structures — poor leadership decisions, poor counseling, adulterous relationships of pastors, and financial impropriety — represents the major factors why people leave churches.[12] This is a heart-breaking fact that many church leaders do not want to face. The consequence of this kind of dysfunction leads to the decline of many churches.

The third issue is related to the often heard phrase, "It just doesn't work for me!" This is a simple explanation given by many church leavers regarding why they leave their churches. When I asked a leader in the Nexus Café Church in Manchester why he left his previous church to be one of the founders of the café church, he said, "It didn't work for me!" This simple expression has profound meaning upon which church leaders ought to ponder. Churches need to know what those aspects are that do not "work" for people.

The fourth issue is a lack of community. Jamieson states after five years of his research that there is great importance in belonging to a faith group. He writes, "It appears that those who do not meet with others in the process of leaving or after leaving are less likely to move on from their faith position at the time of leaving the church."[13] According to Jamieson's research, it is important for churches to build up community for every Christian so that all may have a better chance of remaining in the Church and not become church leavers.

The fifth issue is a lack of a discipleship model. In his book, *The Out of Bounds Church*, Steve Taylor discusses the rise of deconstructionism to push a mentality that God deconstructs.[14] Drane explains the consequence of decon-structionism: "The trend for deconstructing everyone and everything has left us with no heroes to follow, and so most young people are more likely to know what is no longer worth believing in, than to have a positive and clear idea of what they do actually believe."[15] It is difficult to build up models, mentors, and systems because "deconstruction," "negativity," and "no model" are the trend and it is difficult to reverse this wrong direction. Drane asserts that church leaders are too concerned with counting people in the pews in order to prove church growth, while they should be asking, "How much like Christ have we become?"[16] Christ is the only model for believers to follow. It is important that Christians pursue Christlikeness by setting up a countercul-tural model.

The sixth issue is what Drane refers to as a McDonald's-style "fast-food" mentality in the Church. Drane teaches on the trend of doing ministry using a "fast-food style." There are so many pre-packaged models of Christianity to choose from, and this fact has lessened believers' creativity and flexibility: "For if the church offers only the same things as the rationalized world of work, why should people who are oppressed elsewhere in their lives expect to find a resolution by joining the church?"[17] It is difficult for some Christian leaders to understand that they have participated in this kind of fast-food mentality because it has become part of the Christian culture. Quite a number of Christian pastors and leaders have bought pre-packaged materials, trying to copy and paste from some successful megachurches. Some of these mega-church leaders wanted to write a manual for their church-planting strategies, and they let go of an in-depth training process in favor of a "fast-food," rapid-growth style of ministry. Many leaders used to believe that every ministry should be tailor-made, but they are now being "MacDonaldized." The Church must make a u-turn when it comes to this type of ministry.

Christians without a Church

McNeal writes, "A growing number of people are leaving the institutional church for a new reason. They are not leaving because they have lost faith. They are leaving the church to preserve their faith."[18] For centuries, people have been baptized to become members of churches in order to find faith and live their faith. Today, the opposite can occur: people are leaving the Church to preserve their faith. This is a reality and unfortunately many Christians are not paying attention. I know quite a number of Christians who have left their churches due to various painful reasons. They have often formed unofficial small groups and have resisted the idea of returning to a conventional church. They come together for Bible study, prayer, and fellowship, but they generally do not think of themselves as a new church plant.

Taylor writes, "I sit on the fault lines of a cultural shift."[19] I live in Vancouver, British Columbia, Canada, and we really are sitting just twenty miles from the fault lines that cause many minor earthquakes every year. Taylor's words seem like the sound of a siren signaling that an air-raid, a tornado, or an earthquake is coming. And this time it is a cultural earthquake that many church leaders are not aware of.

One cultural shift has brought many people into a mindset that has no interest in eternal life, but Christian leaders are still selling the importance of eternal life. Drane writes, "Today's people are more afraid of living than they are of dying. Who wants to live forever anyway?"[20] Christians today are often enjoying their own church culture, but it may be irrelevant to the mainstream culture. Some other elements of mainstream culture that are affecting people include: a false identity from consumerism; a false identity of the church; and celebrity culture.

A False Identity from Consumerism

Consumerism pushes people to conform and have a false identity. This is ever present in today's culture. It is a culture of disengagement, discontentment, and forgetting. People see things through the dollar sign, and it is the mall and not the church that is important. Getting is more important than giving. We are being taken up with secular consumerism and not challenged by the value of the Gospel. In his lecture for the DMin course, "Creative Pathways in Mission and Ministry for the 21st Century," Drane asserted, "Bible and culture are the key things."[21] Understanding this is the only way to turn this false identity back to the original purpose of our created identity as the *imago Dei*— the image of God.

A False Identity of the Church

The Church is often described as boring, irrelevant, antique, judgmental, and intolerant. It is an accurate picture if believers have the courage to admit it. When people are enjoying the warm fellowship of Christians, it is important to communicate that church life is interesting, relevant, fresh, modern, creative, appreciative, and full of acceptance.

Pioneers and Settlers

In his book, *An Emergent Theology*, Ray Anderson brings out this deep and practical question as the problem of pioneers and settlers: What has Antioch to do with Jerusalem? He states that the real problem is the question regarding apostolic authority: "Paul was never completely accepted by the leaders of the church at Jerusalem as an apostle. But neither did he yield control of the churches that emerged out of Antioch to Jerusalem's apostolic authority."[22] The struggle between Antioch and Jerusalem, between Paul and Peter, between the "Paul-style" evangelists and the "Peter and James-style" conservative church elders has always presented problems within the Church. Pioneers like Paul and settlers like Peter and James are often in conflict with each other and find it very difficult to accept each other's ministries.

As a rector of a large Anglican church and as bishop of twelve churches, I have seen too much of this kind of conflict. Unfortunately, this seems to be a problem that will always be present. Anderson writes, "The church at Jerusalem allowed Christ to come out of the tomb, but one wonders whether they continued to view him as bound with the wrappings with which he was buried."[23] Both pioneer churches as well as settler churches must "unwrap the grave clothes of Lazarus," as Jesus commanded (John 11:43) and let those saved souls walk and begin new lives. For pioneer churches, the "grave clothes" can be represented by the church's moving too fast with church planting, for example. In this situation both clergy and others often become exhausted, burnt out, and pressured to give results regarding numbers of churches planted or attendees. Leaders often lose direction. For settler churches, the "grave clothes" can be represented by spending too much time focused on meetings, maintaining buildings, and all kinds of other administrative burdens. These two very different cultures of churches often make it difficult to work together for a better Kingdom plan for God. When these two types of churches come into contact, there is often misunderstanding, bias, anger, and other negative feelings.

It has been an enormous challenge for many church leaders to determine how the two sides can meet and work together peacefully and joyfully. Drane aptly states that this is a matter of reconciliation: "Our ultimate goal has to be to move on from tolerating diversity, to actively promoting reconciliation. If the Church replicates the fragmentation that is in the world already, it does not deserve to have a future."[24] And reconciliation is impossible without a daily relationship with Jesus. Micro-Macro Discipling is the remedy for this problem that is seemingly impossible to solve.

Celebrity Culture

In his book, *Celebrity Culture*, John Drane discusses the influence of celebrity culture upon people today.[25] He gives an example of a lady he met at a gathering in Hollywood who was telling people that she did not know who she was because her identity was not defined by any inner qualities, but rather by the labels of the clothes she wore. She said that celebrities should stop making the sort of films they are making because these films have robbed her generation of meaningful role models. This seemingly hopeless situation is indeed a fantastic opportunity for advancing the gospel. Celebrities can only offer a glamorous role model for a culture that desperately needs new direction. People's fascination with celebrities expresses their search for meaning and purpose, which is ultimately a search for God.[26] Church leaders today must creatively consider how to redirect this "celebrity-focused culture" from leading people to follow the lifestyles of movie stars to instead follow a lifestyle of Christlikeness. Drane writes, "Like secular celebrities, saints held up a mirror to the culture."[27]

Transfer Growth Rather Than Salvation Growth

According to Ferguson and Ferguson, half of all churches in America did not add one person through conversion in 2009.[28] Christian leaders must admit that when reporting the magnificent growth of some megachurches, this is mostly transfer growth rather than salvation growth. Very few churches have successful ministries to convert non-believers to receive Christ and become Christians. Because of all kinds of known and unknown problems of many churches, Christians like to transfer their membership from one church to another church in a short period of time.

One reason is that people cannot find God in the church. McNeal asserts that the local church has become a religious club, holding meetings where God is conspicuously absent.[29] This is one of the reasons why so many denominations are in decline and why many churches experience transfer growth but not salvation growth. Today's churches are in a new reformation with the goal being to free God's people from this situation.

In a Fuller DMin seminar in England in 2006, professors Yvonne Richmond and Phil Staddon taught that people need basic principles. Because church is thought to be boring, irrelevant, antique, judgmental, and intolerant to many people, people need to encounter simple, basic, and practical principles when they go to church. Unfortunately, as people have moved away from Christianity, they do not understand how to live life even at a basic level. Churches do therefore need to go back and teach the basic elementary principles of life that appear in the Bible before they can teach the deep things of God. Many leaders think that these basic elementary principles of life will be found in a certain program, a system, or anything that works. But "going back to the basics" is a relational pursuit. The basic principle is a relational question challenging one's relationship with Jesus Christ. Without a daily intimate personal relationship with Jesus, there is no hope in building up any other sound ministry.

Summary

There is no kingdom without a king. There is no salvation without a Savior. There is no life without a Lord of life. This is the time that believers need the return of their King, their Savior, and their Lord of life, Jesus Christ, starting with the most micro relational aspect—daily devotion, a daily intimate personal relationship with Jesus. This is the rationale for launching Micro-Macro Discipling because this is the foundation that the world so needs. Without this micro relationship with Jesus, every macro piece of work and ministry will collapse. And indeed, many works and ministries have collapsed. Let us put the foundation back before it is too late.

---

[1] McNeal, *The Present Future*, 1.
[2] Robert Quinn, *Deep Change* (San Francisco: Jossey-Bass, 1996), xiii, 3.
[3] Ibid., xiii.
[4] Ibid., 3.
[5] Cole, *Cultivating a Life for God*, 75.
[6] Willard, *The Divine Conspiracy*, 57.
[7] Dave Ferguson and Jon Ferguson, *Exponential* (Grand Rapids: Zondervan, 2010), 14.

[8] Cole, *Cultivating a Life for God*, 11.

[9] Alan Jamieson, *A Churchless Faith* (London: SPCK, 2002); and Alan Jamieson, Jenny McIntosh, and Adrienne Thompson, *Church Leavers* (London: SPCK, 2006).

[10] Jamieson, *A Churchless Faith*, 142.

[11] Ibid., 4.

[12] Ibid., 44.

[13] Jamieson, McIntosh, and Thompson, *Church Leavers*, 70.

[14] Steve Taylor, *The Out of Bounds Church* (Grand Rapids: Zondervan, 2005), 23.

[15] Drane, *The McDonaldization of the Church*, 64.

[16] Ibid., 41.

[17] Ibid., 31.

[18] McNeal, *The Present Future*, 4.

[19] Taylor, *The Out of Bounds Church*, 19.

[20] John Drane, lecture for the DMin course, "New Ways of Being Church," Fuller Theological Seminary, held in England by Professors John and Olive Drane, May 2008.

[21] Drane, lecture for the DMin course, "New Ways of Being Church."

[22] Ray S. Anderson, *An Emergent Theology* (Downers Grove, IL: InterVarsity, 2006), 205.

[23] Ibid.

[24] Drane, *The McDonaldization of the Church*, 83-84.

[25] John Drane, *Celebrity Culture* (Edinburgh: Rutherford House, 2005).

[26] Ibid., 54-55, 63.

[27] Ibid., 19.

[28] Ferguson and Ferguson, *Exponential*, 14.

[29] McNeal, *The Present Future*, 59.

PART TWO

THEOLOGICAL FOUNDATIONS

CHAPTER FOUR

BIBLICAL DISCIPLESHIP DEVELOPMENT

This chapter discusses four biblical models of discipleship development: John the Baptist's model, Jesus' model, Barnabas's model, and Paul's model. All four models demonstrate the essence of the Micro-Macro Discipleship theory of living out Jesus' parable of the growing seeds from micro discipling to macro church planting. All four models provide vivid examples of how important it is to raise up disciplers, evangelists, mentors, and church planters.[1]

John the Baptist's Model

John the Baptist's discipleship model can be characterized by his "come and see" format of teaching, his one-on-two discipleship strategy, his focus upon Jesus, and his urging of people to repentance. First of all, John the Baptist discipled using a "come and see" method. In John 1:35-42, John the Baptist is with his two disciples, John and Andrew. While he was walking he saw Jesus, and he took that opportunity to have a "come and see" teaching moment (although in this case it was actually "go and see"). He told his two disciples that Jesus was the Lamb of God, which meant Jesus was the long expected Messiah. His disciples heard that and they followed Jesus and stayed with Jesus that night. The next day, Andrew told his elder brother Simon that Jesus was the Messiah, and he brought Simon to see Jesus.

This passage in John 1:35-42 also shows a clear picture of how John the Baptist taught his disciples by having two disciples follow him. This model is a very effective model to train disciples. In another instance John again sends two disciples to ask Jesus a question: "The disciples of John reported all these things to him. And John, calling two of his disciples, sent them to the Lord to ask, 'John the Baptist has sent us to you, saying, "Are you the one who is to come, or shall we look for another?"'" (Luke 7:18-20). This passage demonstrates another example of John's method to train his disciples in groups of two. Later in this chapter it will be seen that Jesus used a similar model with three disciples, namely Peter, James, and John. These three were always in his inner circle of disciples, and Jesus trained them to be three very influential leaders of the early Church.

There is also evidence that John sometimes worked with a group of disciples. In John 3:25-26, the writer reports, "Now a discussion arose between some of John's disciples and a Jew over purification. And they came to John and said to him, "Rabbi, he who was with you across the Jordan, to whom you bore wit-ness—look, he is baptizing, and all are going to him." This mention of this group of John's disciples arguing with a certain Jew over the matter of ceremonial wash-ing shows a kind of small group discipling method.

Another discipleship focus of John the Baptist was that he pointed others to Jesus. The result of John the Baptist's words to John and Andrew that "Jesus is the Lamb of God" was that they followed Jesus right away and then stayed the night with him. With those two days of personal time with Jesus, Andrew found out what he wanted to confirm, that Jesus was the Messiah. Then he rushed home to get his brother Simon to meet Jesus as well. John's way of discipleship was not to build his own kingdom, but rather he was ready to pass his disciples along to Jesus when the time came.

Another passage also indicates that John's ministry points to Jesus the Messi-ah. In John 3:27-36 the author writes,

> John answered, "A person cannot receive even one thing unless it is given him from heaven. You yourselves bear me witness, that I said, 'I am not the Christ, but I have been sent before him.' The one who has the bride is the bridegroom. The friend of the bridegroom, who stands and hears him, rejoices greatly at the bridegroom's voice. Therefore this joy of mine is now complete. He must increase, but I must decrease." He who comes from above is above all. He who is of the earth belongs to the earth and speaks in an earthly way. He who comes from heaven is above all. He bears witness to what he has seen and heard, yet no one receives his testimony. Whoever receives his testimony sets his seal to this, that God is true. For he whom God has sent utters the words of God, for he gives the Spirit without measure. The Father loves the Son and has given all things into his hand. Whoever believes in the Son has eternal life; whoever does not obey the Son shall not see life, but the wrath of God remains on him.

He told his disciples clearly that Jesus must become greater and he must become less. He points to a personal relationship with Jesus the Messiah, and this is a good example of how John wished that more people would believe in Jesus and receive eternal life.

Another mark of John's discipleship was that he urged people to repent. His baptism was a baptism of repentance; sin was confessed; people were baptized; and his mission was accomplished. Matthew 3:1-12 details this aspect:

> In those days John the Baptist came preaching in the wilderness of Judea, "Repent, for the kingdom of heaven is at hand." For this is he who was spoken of by the prophet Isaiah when he said,
>
> "The voice of one crying in the wilderness:
>
> 'Prepare the way of the Lord;
>
> make his paths straight.'"
>
> Now John wore a garment of camel's hair and a leather belt around his waist, and his food was locusts and wild honey. Then Jerusalem and all Judea and all the region about the Jordan were going out to him, and they were baptized by him in the river Jordan, confessing their sins.
>
> But when he saw many of the Pharisees and Sadducees coming to his baptism, he said to them, "You brood of vipers! Who warned you to flee from the wrath to come? Bear fruit in keeping with repentance. And do not presume to say to yourselves, 'We have Abraham as our father,' for I tell you, God is able from these stones to raise up children for Abraham. Even now the axe is laid to the root of the trees. Every tree therefore that does not bear good fruit is cut down and thrown into the fire. I baptize you with water for repentance, but he who is coming after me is mightier than I, whose sandals I am not worthy to carry. He will baptize you with the Holy Spirit and fire. His winnowing fork is in his hand, and he will clear his threshing floor and gather his wheat into the barn, but the chaff he will burn with unquenchable fire."

The Matthew 3:1-12 passage above also exhibits another example of John's discipleship style, which is that he emulated a simple lifestyle. He wore a garment of camel's hair and a leather belt around his waist, and he ate locusts and wild honey. It is likely that John wanted his disciples to imitate and follow this simple lifestyle as well.

Jesus' Model

In several passages in Scripture (including Mark 1:29-39, Luke 6:12-16, Luke 4:38-44, and Luke 5:16) a clear pattern is shown of Jesus' own daily devotion. Jesus' devotional time is also clearly seen as preceding some of his important decisions. In Mark 1, the following passage comes directly after the healing of Peter's mother-in-law and before he tells his disciples that they are moving on. "And rising very early in the morning, while it was still dark, he departed and went out to a desolate place, and there he prayed" (Mark 1:35). Again in Luke 6, the passage referring to Jesus' devotional time directly precedes the important event of his naming the twelve: "In these days he went out to the mountain to pray, and all night he continued in prayer to God. And when day came, he called his disciples and chose from them twelve, whom he named apostles" (Luke 6:12). Evidently, after his intimate personal time with the Father, Jesus found new purpose and direction. Likewise, believers today need to receive direction from the Lord each day in order that they find themselves in God's will, according to God's plan, and glorifying his name.

In addition to his daily devotion being the source of guidance and direction for Jesus, it was also a source of power. In John 5:19-20 Jesus says, "Truly, truly, I say to you, the Son can do nothing of his own accord, but only what he sees the Father doing. For whatever the Father does, the Son does likewise. For the Father loves the Son and shows him all that he himself is doing. And greater works than these will he show him, so that you may marvel." Indeed, powerful and miraculous events occurred directly following Jesus' time along with the Father. In Matthew 14:13, 20-21, the five thousand are fed after Jesus spent time alone with God. In Matthew 14:22-33, Jesus walks on water to his disciples and calms the stormy seas after he has been praying. When Jesus prays with Peter, James, and John on the mountaintop, the transfiguration occurs (Matthew 17:1-9). And finally at Gethsemane, Jesus prays into the night while his disciples sleep, in preparation for his great sacrifice (Matthew 26:36-44).

These five passages reveal a clear picture of how daily devotion became the source of power for Jesus. Jesus could not do anything without seeing what the Father showed him. Without that intimate personal relationship with the Father, Jesus could not have performed those miracles nor faced his own death so obediently. Clearly Jesus did not only spend time with God when he felt a particular need, but his daily devotional experiences caused these miracles to happen.

The purpose of daily devotions is to have an intimate relationship with Jesus. In Luke 24:13-35, two disciples unknowingly converse with Jesus on the road to Emmaus. This passage shows the significance of being with Jesus and having an intimate personal relationship with him. A believer's willingness to stay and be with Jesus daily will provide opportunities each day to experience what the two disciples experience on the road to Emmaus. Their hearts "burned within them" as they spoke with him. Likewise, believers today may also experience a "burning heart" as they understand the Bible. Many Christians have been studying the Bible all their lives, but only on an academic level; a living encounter with Jesus will open their eyes to see what the Lord wants them to see. Believers may also experience a willingness to change course just as the two disciples changed their course from Emmaus back to Jerusalem; similarly God may choose to send prayerful believers in directions that differ from their own goals.

In his book, *Transforming Discipleship*, Greg Ogden discusses the reason and necessity for Jesus to choose only a few disciples to train. He writes, "Jesus focused on a few because that was the way to grow people and ensure transference of his heart and vision to them. This kind of relationship, however, has been lacking in many of our lives."[2] Passages such as Mark 5:35-37, Matthew 17:1-3, and Matthew 26:36-37 demonstrate Jesus' effort to spend most of his time raising up only three disciples. Significantly, all three became top leaders of the early Church. Peter became the leader for the whole early Church; James became the leader of the Church of Jerusalem, representing the traditional Jewish Christian; and John became the oldest apostle who gave certain important messages and hope to the early Church, especially through the Gospel of John, 1 and 2 John, and the Revelation.

Jesus had several circles of discipleship taking place simultaneously. First, as mentioned above, he spent much of his time training his three "inner circle" disciples, namely Peter, James, and John. These three then joined the rest of the twelve to become his middle circle: the twelve apostles. Jesus also had the group of seventy-two disciples as described in Luke 10:1-24, and this group was organized as sets of pairs. Finally there were the 120 disciples who were waiting for the outpouring of the Holy Spirit as described in Acts 1:15. In addition to these circles of discipleship, Jesus also taught the crowds, as evidenced in Luke 19:47-48, Luke 21:37-38, and John 8:1-2. These passages reveal a micro level of

Jesus' discipleship as he encourages the crowds in the discipline of daily devotion.

Another glimpse into Jesus' strategy of discipleship comes not from the records of his own relationships but from one of his parables. In the parable of the seed in Mark 4:26-29, Jesus explains, "This is what the kingdom of God is like. A man scatters seed on the ground. Night and day, whether he sleeps or gets up, the seed sprouts and grows, though he does not know how. All by itself the soil produces grain—first the stalk, then the head, then the full kernel in the head. As soon as the grain is ripe, he puts the sickle to it, because the harvest has come." This strategy starts first with the micro level of the stalk, then the head, then the full kernel in the head, then the harvest. By observing how Jesus demonstrated his pattern to teach his disciples, he started with his daily intimate personal relationship with the Father (the stalk); then he trained his three "inner circle" apostles, Peter, James, and John (the head); then the twelve; then the seventy-two (the full kernel in the head); and finally the early Church as a harvest of millions of Christians.

Following Jesus' model to prepare the good soil as in the parable of the growing seed, the harvest can be thirty, sixty, or even one hundredfold (Mark 4:20). Thirtyfold is a number with nine zeros after one, and one hundredfold is thirty zeros after one. This is what Jesus means for a harvest. Certainly this happened in the early Church, and it has happened in our day as a result of the lives of people like Billy Graham or John Stott. But if there is a major problem at the micro level, everything will be handicapped and may even collapse.

Barnabas's Model

Barnabas used a very traditional, one-on-one, "master and apprentice" model. Two keys words of Barnabas's strategy to train disciples would be "trust" and "encouragement." This section will review Barnabas's experiences discipling Paul and John Mark.

When Paul came to Jerusalem to meet the apostles, it was three years after his conversion (Galatians 1:18), and the apostles most likely had heard about his transformation. Yet he was still refused by the apostles due to his reputation for having persecuted the Church of God (Galatians 1:13). However, Barnabas, being the "son of encouragement" (Acts 4:36), supported Paul before the apostles. Acts 9:27 reports, "But Barnabas took him and brought him to the apostles. He told them how Saul [i.e. Paul] on his journey had seen the Lord and that the Lord

46

had spoken to him, and how in Damascus he had preached fearlessly in the name of Jesus." It is important to note that Barnabas did not say, "Paul *said* that he had seen the Lord and that the Lord had spoken to him" or "I have *heard* that Paul had seen the Lord." Barnabas told the apostles what happened to Paul as if he had himself been an eyewitness. He completely trusted Paul and pledged his own goodwill on him. By doing so, Barnabas helped Paul to integrate with the Church and the apostles in Jerusalem, and showed him an excellent example of trust in other disciples.

Later, when Paul's life was in danger due to his preaching, the apostles sent him back to Tarsus (Acts 9:30), where Paul worked on his own for the next ten years. Ten years after Paul left Jerusalem, Barnabas wanted to have a helper and he thought of Paul. He went to Tarsus to look for him (Acts 11:25). Barnabas worked with Paul together in Tarsus for one year. He then left Tarsus with Paul to go to Jerusalem. This was fourteen years after Paul had gone to Jerusalem initially (Galatians 2:1).

After their work in Jerusalem, Barnabas and Paul went back to Tarsus together. There, they were sent out on their first missionary journey (Acts 13:3). Barnabas and Paul worked together very closely during the whole journey. In the beginning, Barnabas most likely led Paul and showed him what to do in most of the gatherings. This is inferred by the fact that when both of their names are mentioned, Barnabas's name always precedes Paul's (Acts 11:30, 12:25, 13:1, 13:2, 13:7, 14:14, 15:12, 15:25). Later, when Paul was doing most of the speaking, the sequence changed to Paul's name first and then Barnabas's in most instances (Acts 13:42, 13:43, 13:46, 13:50, 14:1, 14:3, 14:23, 15:2, 15:22, 15:35, 15:36). Yet even when Paul did most of the speaking, Barnabas was supporting him, watching out for him, and encouraging him. Their roles are indirectly revealed in the knowledge that Barnabas was called Zeus, the father of gods in Greek mythology, and Paul was called Hermes, the chief speaker (Acts 14:12). This kind of discipleship training made it possible for Paul to work without Barnabas during the rest of the missionary journeys.

Barnabas used the same one-on-one strategy with John Mark, trusting him and encouraging him in the midst of his strained relationship with Paul. Despite having not had much experience in ministry and his timid character (Mark 14:51), John Mark was brought by Barnabas and Paul from Jerusalem to Antioch, and then on their first missionary journey (Acts 12:25). John Mark played the role of assisting Barnabas and Paul during the first missionary journey (Acts 13:5).

There, Barnabas discipled John Mark and built him up as a church leader for the future. But due to his weak character, John Mark left Barnabas and Paul and went back to Jerusalem in the middle of the first missionary journey (Acts 13:5).

When Barnabas started on the second missionary journey, he communicated his desire to bring John Mark along to give him a second chance after he had deserted Paul and Barnabas. This caused a serious conflict between Barnabas and Paul (Acts 15:36-40). Barnabas, showing his usual character as the "son of encouragement" (Acts 4:36), insisted on bringing John Mark along even though that caused Paul and Barnabas to go their separate ways. This unwittingly conformed to God's plan for a wider spread of the gospel.

Although Paul had ill feelings towards John Mark after the first missionary journey (Acts 15:38), he recognized John Mark as being a great leader of the Church after he had worked with Barnabas and other apostles. When Paul was in prison, he requested the company of John Mark (2 Timothy 4:11), and John Mark stayed with Paul for some time (Colossians 4:10, Philemon 24). John Mark's recognition by Paul was mentioned in various letters by Paul (2 Timothy 4:11). John Mark's work was also recognized by Peter, who called him "my son" in 1 Peter 5:13. It is also believed that the Gospel of Mark was written by John Mark.

Paul's Model

As Paul himself was discipled by Barnabas, he himself discipled many others. In Scripture, the reader can glimpse Paul's style of discipleship by noting his relationships with Silas, Timothy, and the leaders of the church in Ephesus. Each of these discipleship relationships provides insight into Paul's personal model.

Silas

Paul used what he learned from Barnabas—the one-on-one method and also the importance of trust and encouragement—in his discipleship of Silas. Silas was already a very gifted person before he met Paul. He had the gift of prophecy (Acts 15.32) and he was considered one of the apostles (Acts 15:22). Along with Judas, Silas was appointed by the apostles to accompany Barnabas and Paul for a mission to Antioch. After the mission had been accomplished, Silas remained in Antioch (Acts 15:34) where Paul was as well (Acts 15:35).

When Paul started his second missionary journey after parting ways with Barnabas, he chose Silas to go with him (Acts 15:40). This was a very long journey, both time-wise and geographically. From a geographic point of view, the journey started in Antioch, then the team went to Syria (Acts 15:40), Cilicia (Acts 15:40), Troas (Acts 16:8), Samothrace (Acts 16:11), Neapolis (Acts 16:11), Philippi (Acts 16:12), Amphipolis (Acts 17:1), Thessalonica (Acts 17:1), and Berea (Acts 17:11). There, Paul was forced to go on his own to Athens and then to Corinth (Acts 18:11), where Silas rejoined him. Thereafter, Paul left Corinth but Silas remained there (Acts 18:18). The entire journey spanned several years. In Corinth alone, the team stayed for eighteen months (Acts 18:11).

During this journey, Paul and Silas were always together. In Acts, their names were mentioned together nine times (Acts 16:19, 16:22 16:25, 16:29, 16:38, 16:40, 17:4, 17:5, 17:10). By working together so closely, Paul had many opportunities to demonstrate to Silas how to preach the gospel and how to live a simple lifestyle. On the other hand, Silas was such a great helper to Paul that when Paul was forced to go to Athens on his own, he immediately "instructed Silas and Timothy to join him as soon as possible" (Acts 17:15). In the letters to the churches, Paul often mentioned Silas's name, thus reconfirming Silas's importance to him (2 Corinthians 1:19, 1 Thessalonians 1:1, 2 Thessalonians 1:1). Such mention likely gave encouragement and recognition to Silas in his work, which would have been a great incentive for Silas to work harder still.

Timothy

Paul invited Timothy to join him and Silas on his second missionary journey. This means that Paul was at some points discipling two individuals in a "one-on-two" model, as John the Baptist and Jesus also did. Paul identified Timothy as a potential apprentice. He invited him to come along and gave him on-the-job training (Acts 16:2-3). Paul then provided an opportunity for Timothy to practice what he had learned from Paul by sending Timothy ahead of him to Macedonia (Acts 19:22).

Paul intentionally built a strong relationship with Timothy and called him "my fellow worker" (Romans 16:21). In doing so he gave him authority by publicly including Timothy in his ministry (1 Corinthians 4:17; 2 Corinthians 1:19). Paul also set clear expectations for Timothy that as a leader he ought to be a slave of Christ (Philippians 1:1). Paul completely trusted Timothy to do ministry, affirming him to be the leader (Philippians 2:19-20; 1 Thessalonians 3:2) as well as affirming his relationship with Timothy as spiritual father and son (Philippians 2:22; 1 Timothy 1:2, 18). Paul gave clear instructions to Timothy regarding his ministry (1 Timothy 1:18; 6:2, 11, 20) and reminded him that all resources came from God's grace (1 Timothy 1:2; 2 Timothy 1:2-3). Paul also gave Timothy clear instructions and warning about the fact that difficult times would come (2 Timothy 3:1).

Leaders in Ephesus

Paul's first time in Ephesus was mentioned in Acts 18:19: "They arrived in Ephesus…He himself went into the synagogue and reasoned with the Jews." Yet this time he could not stay long there. However, when he left, he promised that "I [Paul] will come back if it is God's will" (Acts 18:21). Finally, he did return to Ephesus, which demonstrated that it was indeed God's will for him to be there.

When Paul was in Ephesus the second time (Acts 19:1), he started the training with the most basic fact: the need of baptism in the name of Jesus (Acts 19:5) so that they could receive the Holy Spirit (Acts 19:6). These leaders needed the very basic yet imperative element, the Holy Spirit, in order to start with the Lord's work. The need of this baptism was also mentioned in some of the Paul's letters (1 Corinthians 12:13).

Paul started the training by confining the number of leaders in a small group to no more than twelve (Acts 19:7). He then left the synagogue because the people refused to believe and publicly maligned "the Way" (Acts 19:9). At this point he established the school of Tyrannus (Acts 19:9). This went on for two years so that every person could have a chance to hear the Word of the Lord (Acts 19:10), and this school became the training centre for many missionaries. In this way, the leaders of Ephesus were able to stay with Paul and learn from him for almost three years. The leaders could also see and be encouraged by the results of Paul's work that "the word of the Lord spread widely and grew in power" (Acts 19:20).

When Paul left Ephesus, he gave his encouragement to the leaders and other Jesus followers (Acts 20:1). After Paul left Ephesus, all the works in Ephesus were in the sole hands of the leaders there. Even though Paul was in a great hurry, and did not have time to enter Ephesus, he asked the leaders (elders) of Ephesus to go to see him in Miletus (Acts 20:17). As Paul thought that he would not see those leaders anymore (Acts 20:38), he spent the "final" time with them in Miletus giving them encouragement and exhortation. He reminded the leaders of what he had taught during the previous three years with them (Acts 20:31), and what he, as their leader, had shown them to do (Acts 20:35). He reminded them that he had passed on all of his knowledge to them (Acts 20:27). He reminded them of their responsibility and rights as leaders in Ephesus as they were authorized directly by the Holy Spirit to be the overseers (Acts 20:28). He reassured the leaders that even though he himself would not be with them anymore, God, who is much mightier than Paul, would be with them always. He said, "I commit you [the leaders] to God and to the word of his grace, which can build you up" (Acts 20:32).

Summary

This chapter has addressed the biblical foundations for discipleship development according to the models of John the Baptist, Jesus, Barnabas, and Paul. Based upon these examples, daily devotion and discipling in a biblical context are certainly important. These discipling examples demonstrate the necessity of Christian formation on the micro and the macro level, as in the four stages of the growing seed and the reality of a harvesting one hundredfold. Through their examples, John the Baptist, Jesus, Barnabas, and Paul demonstrate this "micro to macro" way of discipleship by their lifestyles and witness.

---

[1] See Appendix G for an image depicting the model.

[2] Greg Ogden, *Transforming Discipleship* (Downers Grove, IL: InterVarsity Press, 2003), 73.

CHAPTER FIVE

ECCLESIOLOGICAL DISCIPLESHIP DEVELOPMENT

This chapter addresses the ecclesiological foundations for discipleship development at various stages in the history of the Church. The early Church Christians demonstrated a very special lifestyle of Christlikeness, as did the Christians in the Celtic Church. The Church has much to unlearn so that all of its members can establish a daily intimate personal relationship with Jesus as part of healthy discipleship development.

The Early Church Model

In his book, *Revolution in Leadership,* Reggie McNeal states that the success of many churches is due to their willingness to go back to the early Church model. He writes,

> The call in the church today is for apostolic leadership. What does "apostolic" mean? What significance compels its use for describing the kind of leadership the church needs for the future? Why recall the past when considering how to embrace the twenty-first century?

> These questions can be answered with three assertions. First, the dynamic of the early church during the apostolic era remains a benchmark for missional effectiveness. Second, the cultural arena at the beginning of the twenty-first century resembles at key points the cultural setting that first-century Christians faced. Third, and most significantly, the type of leadership the apostles practiced possesses certain qualities that not only made the early church effective but would raise the level of church leadership today as we face similar challenges and opportunities.[1]

The early Church was effective due to a model of apostolic leadership that led to missional effectiveness, and due to certain leadership qualities that the apostles practiced. The Church today desperately needs to raise the level of church leadership in such a way. The Church needs apostolic leaders to help today's Church return to its original call of being a body of Christ.

Characteristics of Apostolic Leaders

McNeal describes several characteristics of first-century church leaders. He explains that the leaders were visionary, missional, empowering, team-oriented and reproducing, entrepreneurial, and kingdom-conscious. Each quality worked together to create an effective ministry.

First of all, they were visionary. McNeal writes, "Early church leaders gave their lives in pursuit of a compelling vision of the kingdom of God that Jesus shared with them...Not only do they possess a personal vision that grips them, they know how to bring others on board with them to work for its realization. Such leaders realize that leading their congregations to do business as usual will not qualify as obedience to the Lord."[2] Apostolic leaders are those leaders who can receive a kingdom plan from Jesus, share this plan with their membership, and put it into practice. Unfortunately, many church leaders do ministry in a "business as usual" way, which leads to stagnation.

In my personal experience, I received a vision from Jesus two months before I became a bishop when I prayed and asked the Lord what he wanted me to do as an apostle. The Lord asked me to do what the apostles did in Acts 6:4, "We will give our attention to prayer and the ministry of the word." This project is one outcome of that vision: the development of a simple, focused, and deep model using a four-year plan to lead the sixteen churches under my jurisdiction back to the early Church apostolic movement which I have called micro discipleship.

Second, the apostles of the early Church were missional. McNeal discusses the missional focus of today's apostolic leaders: "Today's apostolic leaders are freshly challenging the church to evaluate its attitudes and activities in light of Jesus' last command before returning to the Father. These paradigm pioneers are practicing intentionality in their ministries that shows up in kingdom expansion. They courageously refuse to let their congregations settle for maintenance ministry."[3] For leaders of Anglican churches, it is difficult to refuse to let congregations settle for maintenance ministry. For too many Anglican churches, retaining the same number of average Sunday attendance is a success; to have an increase in attendance would be a special case; and to plant a new church would be a miracle. To be a missional church is a challenge as well as a mandate from the Lord to apostolic leaders. The four-year plan in this project demonstrates the fruit of our willingness to become a missional church.

Third, the early Church apostles were empowering. McNeal recounts the decision on the part of the early Church apostles to expand leadership:

> As the number of early believers multiplied, the apostles made a strategic decision. They opted to share the ministry with others outside their immediate leadership circle (Acts 6:1-6). This risky move paid off.\The church ministry entered a new era of expansion (Acts 6:7)...Effective church leaders today understand that the strategic way to leverage their ministry efforts is to empower others to minister...They release the ministry from being bottle-necked in the hands of a few "professionals."[4]

McNeal explains that the empowering process is a risky move, but it paid off for the early Church and it will pay off in our time as well. Unfortunately, many clergy and pastors do not know how to empower their leaders and other lay people to minister. Often, clergy and pastors do not know how to "lower the bar" so that more people can have a chance to serve. It is like eighty thousand people watching a soccer match with only twenty-two players running like mad on the field.

Fourth, the early Church apostles were team-oriented and reproducing. McNeal explains how this was the reality of the early Church:

> Jesus had his Twelve. The early Jerusalem church was led by a senior team including some trained by the Master. Paul developed...Timothy, Luke, Silas, Barnabas, John Mark, and Titus. The apostles practiced team leadership and trained people to reproduce local leadership teams. New apostolic leaders practice and reproduce a leadership that is plural in its essence and expression. This new model moves beyond the CEO approach with its attendant tensions and trappings. Apostolic leaders of the future will make leadership development a priority of their ministry. They will know how to recruit and coach others into leadership excellence. Their legacy will be the quality of leaders they leave behind.[5]

Apostolic leaders need to make leadership development a priority of their ministries. Team ministry and the ability to reproduce those teams is a great challenge. Apostolic leaders today need to produce other high quality leaders as did

Jesus, Paul, and the other leaders of the early Church so that kingdom growth will become a reality and not merely a dream.

Fifth, the early Church apostles were entrepreneurial. McNeal writes,

> The early church leaders were entrepreneurs in the classic sense of this word (those who organize, manage, and assume risk for a venture). They assumed stewardship of the Christian movement under the leadership of the Holy Spirit, who is the ultimate Entrepreneur. The apostles cooperated with the Spirit to rapidly expand their market. They knew how to connect the gospel with their culture...Emerging apostolic leaders take their cues from cultural exegesis in addition to their biblical insights. They take full advantage of opportunities for sharing the gospel in ways that unchurched people find appealing. This approach will involve far more ministry outside church walls. It necessitates a shift in thinking that begins to look for ways God is at work in the world, not just for what he is doing in the church. Rather than dreaming up church programs and then trying to attract people to them, apostolic leaders begin with their insights into people's needs and then design ministry efforts to meet them where they are.[6]

How well leaders can organize, manage, and assume risk for a venture determines whether they will be successful entrepreneurs like the leaders of the early Church. Few leaders in today's Church possess these kinds of qualities; few can think "out of the box" and create ministries outside the church walls. This will be quite a challenge for church leaders today to become and to raise up successful entrepreneurs.

Finally, the early Church apostles were kingdom-conscious. Moving away from "churchianity" back to Christianity is McNeal's appeal to all Christians:

> Early believers had to overcome a religious background informed by Judaism's exclusivism. Explosive growth occurred once they understood that the gospel was for everyone and God could be served in new ways. The leaders focused on reaching people in obedience to Christ, not on developing an institution. Not until old sacerdotal values reasserted themselves among leaders in the second and third centuries did kingdom concerns give way to institutional church concerns.

Today's new apostolic leaders are determined to prosecute a kingdom agenda for God's people. They are determined to follow Christ out into the world where they can dispel some darkness with his light. They join ranks with other believers to put Christianity into action in their communities. Those who can move beyond the constraints of "churchianity" discover an explosion of kingdom growth waiting to occur.[7]

Many Christian leaders have been focused on learning and practicing church growth, but kingdom growth is what Jesus and the early Church apostles focused on and worked towards.

McNeal's insights regarding the characteristics of apostolic leaders invites church leaders today to re-examine how well they understand the power of the early Church and how can they can become apostolic leaders. Each characteristic serves as a check point for one's goal to become an apostolic leader and one's ministry to raise up apostolic leaders.

The Intentional Process of Developing a Learning Community

The intentional process of developing a learning community is also part of the essence of the early Church model of being church. McNeal writes,

> A new learning paradigm is emerging for leaders: the learning community. One definition of a learning community reads like this: A group of colleagues who come together in a spirit of mutual respect, authenticity, learning, and shared responsibility to continually explore and articulate an expanding awareness and base of knowledge. The process of a learning community includes inquiring about each other's assumptions and biases, experimenting, risking, and openly assessing the results.
>
> Does this sound familiar? Reflect again on the apostolic era. With the whole world to save, Jesus decided to create a learning community. He called a group together to share a journey and to learn from him the most incredible truths ever revealed to humanity. The apostles watched and listened as Jesus worked and taught. They debriefed together the experiences they shared. Jesus sent them out on mission and unpacked their experiences when they returned. Along the way he challenged their notions about what God was up to in the world.[8]

Following this model, today's churches need to become learning communities. Churches may not understand the importance of developing learning communities. But it is clear that many Christian leaders are experiencing burnout because they are "doing" ministry without the support and nurture of learning communities.

APEPT Model

Michael Frost and Alan Hirsch, in their book, *The Shaping of Things to Come*, present another way of looking at apostolic leaders in terms of the fivefold ministry described in Ephesians 4:1-16.[9] They call their model the APEPT model, based upon the fivefold ministry: Apostle, Prophet, Evangelist, Pastor, and Teacher. Frost and Hirsch give an example using the Apostle Paul:

> Paul actually sees APEPT ministry as the very mechanism for achieving mission and ministry effectiveness and Christian maturity. He seems to be saying that without a fivefold ministry pattern we cannot mature. If this is true, it is impossible to estimate what terrible damage the church has done through the loss, even active suppression, of this crucial dimension of New Testament ministry and leadership. But if we take these verses at face value, then it is our contention that the impact has been significant indeed. Perhaps the fact that APEPT has not been intentionally nurtured and practiced might have something to do with the immaturity we find in the Western church that inhibits fulfillment of its mission.[10]

Frost and Hirsch theorize that a missional-apostolic church will only flourish under APEPT leadership. They believe that it will take the emergence of the pioneering-missional type of leader to accomplish this. But they also contend that the western Church simply does not have enough of the apostolic, prophetic, and evangelistic leaders at present to get the job of mission done.[11] ACiC has been working on this aspect to restore this APEPT ministry. The four-year plan in this book develops a strategy to raise up apostles (as in church planters), evangelists, pastors (as in disciplers), teachers (as in mentors/coaches), and prophets (as in prayer warriors).

A Lifestyle of Christlikeness

In his book, *The Spirit of the Disciplines,* Willard contends that the early Christians arranged their lives very differently from non-Christians. He writes,

> Wherever early Christians looked they saw examples of the practice of solitude, fasting, prayer, private study, communal study, worship, and sacrificial service and giving—to mention only some of the more obvious disciplines for spiritual life. These early Christians really did arrange their lives very differently from their non-Christian neighbors, as well as from the vast majority of those of us called Christians today. We are speaking of their overall style of life, not just what they did under pressure, which frequently was also astonishingly different.[12]

Stott uses one word to summarize this kind of lifestyle of early Church Christians: Christlikeness. When I visited John Stott in July 2009 he told me, "Silas, if you want to ask me what is the most important thing in my life and I have only one word, it is 'Christlikeness.'" Christians of the early Church truly lived out a lifestyle of Christlikeness which, as Willard declares, "the vast majority of those of us called Christians today" do not.[13]

Stott explains that the early Church model leads to a lifestyle of Christlikeness. He states clearly that the early Church in Acts 2 was a learning church, a loving church, a worshipping church, and an evangelistic church.[14] But to many people, including Christians, the Church has become the opposite: non-teachable, without love, characterized by boring worship, and without evangelization. The challenge for leaders today is to turn all of this around.

The Celtic Model

Most Anglican churches in North America have fewer than one hundred people in attendance at their Sunday services, and these churches would like to grow. George Hunter, in his book, *The Celtic Way of Evangelism,* provides a clear understanding of how the Celtic way can inform churches today regarding how to bring people to Christ. He writes, "Patrick and his people launched a movement...His mission planted about 700 churches, and Patrick ordained perhaps 1000 priests. Within his lifetime, 30 to 40 (or more) of Ireland's 150 tribes became substantially Christian...Patrick seized the high ground to serve in 'apostolic succession,' that is, to succeed the ancient apostles in their mission to pre-Christian populations."[15] Hunter presents five themes of the Celtic missionary ecclesiology: team evangelization, monastic training, good prayer life, hospitality, and the Celtic fellowship. Each of these themes offers guidance to churches today regarding discipleship development.[16] The five themes about "missionary ecclesiology" from the ancient Celtic Christian movement are so simple and practical that, if followed, should help churches grow.

The first theme of Celtic missionary ecclesiology is team evangelization. I visited a rector of a medium-sized church in Texas a few years ago. We went to seminary together in the eighties and since then we have been good friends. He expressed how frustrated and burned out he was and that he wanted to quit. When I asked him questions about his leadership style, it became clear that he is a "Lone Ranger" type of leader, as Hunter describes. He did not know how to develop team ministries or team evangelization. This "Lone Ranger" mentality leads to defeat for many pastors and leaders. Church leaders today desperately need to restore the Celtic strategy of team evangelization.

The second theme of Celtic missionary ecclesiology is monastic training. Monastic training is a way in which the monastic community prepared people to live with depth, compassion, and power in mission. Nowadays Christians are often shallow, without compassion, and without power in mission. Many Christian leaders are stuck, but have no clue how to get out of the mud.

The third theme of Celtic missionary ecclesiology is a good prayer life. The Celtic model involves imaginative prayer in various settings—solitude, soul friend, small group, corporate life, and ministry with seekers. Nowadays, many pastors and Christians are busy in their marketing strategies to promote complicated methods in discipleship formation and church planting. But the basic need to establish a good prayer life is truly the essence of what is needed. The strategy for micro discipleship is based upon this simple truth of daily devotional time (which essentially is synonymous with a good prayer life), and so far it has been successful in all sixteen churches in the ACiC.

The fourth theme of Celtic missionary ecclesiology is hospitality. The role of the monastic community's hospitality in ministry with seekers, visitors, refugees, and other guests is a great inspiration for today's Christians. Many churches have tried to launch effective programs for seekers, but it is not easy for non-Christians to feel welcome. The Alpha Program is a good example of how to exercise hospitality in a real sense. Churches must find concrete ways of teaching members about the gift of hospitality.

The fifth theme of Celtic missionary ecclesiology is conversion as a process. Hunter describes this as "helping people to belong so that they can believe."[17] This is exactly the opposite of how many churches have been working on the process of conversion, which is to help people to believe so they can belong. They are first invited to an evangelistic meeting, and once they receive Christ they will be placed in a small group to start a process of Christian formation. But the Celtic model operates differently and proved to be very effective. In addition to the Alpha course, there are other "programs" that follow the Celtic model and should be used today. Discipler 123 and Life Transformation Groups are two of these, and they will be discussed in Part Three of this book.

In addition to the five themes of Celtic missionary ecclesiology, Hunter's thoughts regarding how churches need to be recovery communities is significant for today's North American culture. He writes, "A host of New Barbarians substantially populate the Western world once again; indeed, they are all around us...These populations are increasingly similar to the populations that the movements of Patrick reached...Most churches assume that the postmodern New Barbarians are unreachable because they are not 'civilized' enough to become 'real' Christians."[18] Many Christians do not understand that there are more and more people outside of the Church who have not heard the name Jesus. Instead, many Christians are still working in a kind of "church culture" mentality, despite the fact that church culture is no longer the norm of western society.

The Anglican Model

In their book, *The Oxford Guide to the Book of Common Prayer*, Charles Hefling and Cynthia Shattuck describe the importance of the daily office (that is, daily prayer) within the Anglican tradition. They write,

> The root of the Prayer Book's Daily Office lies deep in antiquity. Daily prayer in the morning, evening, and at night was a feature of Judaism. Early Christianity appears to have retained this practice from its Jewish roots, though other hours were added as well. Eventually, morning and evening emerged as the most important times to pray. Such prayer was not the responsibility of particular kinds of Christians such as monastics (which did not yet exist), clergy, or the particularly

pious, but was the responsibility of all Christians, whether alone or in small groups.[19]

For centuries, Anglicans have participated in daily devotion in two ways, either by going to church for the daily office or by saying the daily office using the Book of Common Prayer at home. For the three years when I was studying my MDiv at Nashotah House, I did not need to have daily devotion because we had a 7:30 am Eucharist and a 5 pm Evensong. We participated in corporate worship and private devotion together. Stephen Sykes, John Booty, and Jonathan Knight, in their book, *The Study of Anglicanism*, reflect upon the history of the Book of Common Prayer:

> Within Anglicanism the influence of the Bible was channeled and reinforced by the influence of a second book, scarcely less important in the formulation of Anglican tradition: the Book of Common Prayer. It was the genius of Cranmer to bring together into a single volume many different things: the texts necessary for the Sunday Eucharist, the tests for the daily office, the services for ordination, the occasional offices which accompany the believer from birth to burial. Thus there was, in the hands of any churchman who could read, a book which linked private with public prayer, which showed the Bible as a text to be used in worship, and which embraced the whole range of human life, personal as well as social. It represented a balanced and inclusive vision of Christian prayer and worship.[20]

The gospel of Luke records instances of Jesus himself teaching in the temple daily, and it is inferred that he was using the special time of the daily prayer of Judaism:

> And he was teaching daily in the temple. The chief priests and the scribes and the principal men of the people were seeking to destroy him, but they did not find anything they could do, for all the people were hanging on his words. (Luke 19:47-48)

> And every day he was teaching in the temple, but at night he went out and lodged on the mount called Olivet. And early in the morning all the people came to him in the temple to hear him. (Luke 21:37-38)

Jesus was teaching people the real meaning and power of daily devotion. They were spending time with Jesus daily, listening to him, and obeying him through reading God's Word.

It is important to consider whether or not the daily office of the Book of Common Prayer is still a helpful tool for daily devotion for believers today. In my own experience after using the daily office for several years, I realized that it did not help me to have an intimate personal relationship with Jesus. Though it may be helpful for many Anglicans, there are others who need to have a more simple, focused, and deep way of daily devotion. The hope in daily devotion is that Jesus can talk to us, teach us, and be with us, just as he was with the people whom Luke describes.

The Anglican model of discipleship development in the daily office is certainly in need of rejuvenation. In *Deep Change*, Quinn describes such a situation: "The process of formalization initially makes the organization more efficient or effective. As time goes on, however, these routine patterns move the organization toward decay and stagnation. The organization loses alignment with the changing, external reality. As a result, customers go elsewhere for their products and services, and the organization loses its critical resources."[21] Unfortunately, many Anglican leaders do not know that the Church is stuck in this "old paradigm" model; even if they are aware, they do not know how to shift into a new paradigm. In his book, *Leadership Next*, Eddie Gibbs aptly writes, "The biggest hurdles facing long-time leaders may not be in learning new insights and skills, but in unlearning what they consider to be tried and true and what thus provides them with a false sense of security."[22] As an Anglican since birth, I have quite a lot to unlearn and it has been a difficult process. The unlearning process is like the "disc cleanup" and "disc defragmentation" process for a computer. It is not an easy experience, but it will free up time and energy to focus on what is truly important.

"Come to Us as We Are" Mindset

The Anglican model includes a traditional church "Come to us as we are" mindset rather than a "We'll come to you" mindset. This "Come to us as we are" is like furniture that is sold "as is"; the "customer" (in this case, the church visitor) can take it or leave it, but it is what it is. It would be difficult for a traditional Anglican church to move to the "We'll come to you" mindset because the Church has such deep and long-standing traditions. Michael Moynagh, in his book, *Emerging*

Church Introduction, states that a mindset should be like a heartbeat rather than a formula in that it should be more tentative, experimental, and varied.[23] This is a difficult shift for many Anglicans to make, and it will certainly become another big challenge for Anglicans.

Summary

This chapter addresses the ecclesiological foundations for discipleship development at various stages in the history of the Church. The Church has much to unlearn so that all of its members can establish a daily intimate personal relationship with Jesus as part of healthy discipleship development.

---

[1] Reggie McNeal, *Revolution in Leadership* (Nashville: Abingdon, 1998), 19.

[2] Ibid., 28.

[3] Ibid.

[4] Ibid., 28-29.

[5] Ibid., 29.

[6] Ibid., 29-30.

[7] Ibid., 30.

[8] Ibid., 50.

[9] Michael Frost and Alan Hirsch, *The Shaping of Things to Come* (Peabody, MA: Hendrickson, 2003), 165-81.

[10] Ibid., 169.

[11] Ibid., 180.

[12] Dallas Willard, *The Spirit of the Disciplines* (New York: Harper SanFrancisco, 1988), 100.

[13] Ibid.

[14] John Stott, *The Message of Acts* (Leicester, UK: InterVarsity Press, 1990), 82-87.

[15] George C. Hunter, *The Celtic Way of Evangelism* (Nashville: Abingdon Press, 2000), 23-24.

[16] Ibid., 47-55.

[17] Ibid.

[18] Ibid.

[19] Charles Hefling and Cynthia Shattuck, eds., *The Oxford Guide to the Book of Common Prayer* (Oxford: University Press, 2006), 451.

[20] Stephen Sykes, John Booty, and Jonathan Knight, *The Study of Anglicanism* (London: SPCK, 1988), 353.

[21] Quinn, *Deep Change*, 5.

[22] Eddie Gibbs, *Leadership Next* (Downers Grove, IL: InterVarsity Press, 2005), 35.

[23] Michael Moynagh, *Emerging Church Introduction* (Oxford: Monarch, 2004), 25.

CHAPTER SIX

THEOLOGICAL DISCIPLESHIP DEVELOPMENT

In *The Spirit of the Disciplines*, Willard's wisdom sets the tone of this chapter, which presents the theology of incarnation as the essence of micro discipleship. He writes, "'Theology' is a stuffy word, but it should be an everyday one. That's what practical theology does. It makes theology a practical part of life. A theology is only a way of thinking about and understanding—or misunderstanding—God. Practical theology studies the manner in which our actions interact with God to accomplish his ends in human life."[1] It is through practical theology that the significance of micro discipleship can be understood in the process of discipleship development.

This chapter consists of two parts. The first part discusses the Great Commission as the primary focus of Jesus' incarnation, and that the micro part of Micro-Macro Discipling becomes the missing DNA of what is missing in the Great Commission. The second part considers the meaning of micro discipleship in the context of the practical theology of the incarnation. It consists of three stages: connecting, relationship, and unity. It states the need for the inter-relationship between mentoring and daily devotion to attain what Jesus cares about most—unity—according to John 17.

The Great Commission: Theology of Incarnation

Dan Kimball, in *The Emerging Church*, quotes Mahatma Gandhi in order to provide a true picture of what is wrong in today's Church: Ghandi said, "I like Jesus, but I don't like Christians. Your Christians are so unlike your Christ."[2] Unfortunately, many Christians do not live like Christ and there is no incarnation in many Christians' lives. Stott writes, "We are to be like Christ in his incarnation, in his service, in his love, in his endurance, and in his mission."[3] Before becoming like Christ in his incarnation, Christians must know what incarnation really is.

What Incarnation Is

Thomas Torrance states that the incarnation starts with Christology, and the task of Christology is about how Christ chooses to know each individual so that each one can know him as his or her personal Saviour and Lord. Torrance writes,

It is only when we actually know Christ, know him as our personal saviour and Lord, that we know that we have not chosen him but that he has chosen us; that it is not in our own capacity to give ourselves the power to know him; that it is not in virtue of our own power or our own capacity that he gives us to know him, but in virtue of his power to reveal himself to us and to enable us to know him; that is, faith itself is the gift of God.[4]

By the grace of God believers have a personal relationship with Jesus as Lord, and by faith they are drawn closer and closer to him. Being in relationship with him leads one to become more Christlike, and in turn people see Christ within believers, and they can receive Christ Jesus as their Saviour and Lord too.

Frost and Hirsch have a similar idea regarding incarnation. They explain that it is the process of a personal spiritual journey of knowing Christ so that believers can "be Christ" to those who do not yet know him. Frost and Hirsch write,

> The missional church is incarnational, not attractional, in its ecclesiology. By incarnational we mean it does not create sanctified spaces into which unbelievers must come to encounter the gospel. Rather, the missional church disassembles itself and seeps into the cracks and crevices of a society in order to be Christ to those who don't yet know him…We believe the missional genius of the church can only be unleashed when there are foundational changes made to the church's very DNA.[5]

Frost and Hirsch state that 95 percent of the churches in the West operate in a non-incarnational mode of mission, but rather in an attractional mode. In an attractional model, church members seek to attract unbelievers into church, where they can experience God. But, Frost and Hirsh contend, the attractional model does not work anymore; seekers today will be reached by an incarnational model of church that is a dynamic set of relationships, friendships, and acquaintances.[6] Frost and Hirsch state that the Church today needs a foundational change in this process of knowing Christ and being Christ. Churches must become missional churches because Christendom has moved Christianity into a maintenance mode.[7] Many churches have been in a maintenance mode for years, some even hundreds of years, and it is hoped that they do not go back to the maintenance mode again. There is a missing element of DNA in the process of being a missional and incarnational church: this missing piece is micro discipleship.

Frost and Hirsch describe well the meaning of the incarnation as it relates to micro discipleship:

> The Incarnation is an event in heaven as well as on earth. In Jesus, God meets each of us personally. Henceforth all people, whoever they are and whenever or wherever they live, have the possibility of a personal relationship with God...We believe the Incarnation should inform our mission in God's world—how we, as the fruit of God's Incarnation, should ourselves be and become incarnational.[8]

First, incarnation means a personal relationship with God. Second, because of this personal relationship with God, people's lives bear the fruits of becoming incarnational. The whole world desperately needs to see Christians becoming incarnational—they need to see how Christians' lifestyles and witness reflect that Jesus is Saviour and Lord of life.

What Is Primary

Willard asserts that what characterizes most local congregations, whether big or little in size, is simple distraction. He challenges his readers to consider why the New Testament says nothing about all those matters to which most congregations today devote almost all of their time and effort. Willard contends that those matters are not primary and will take care of themselves with little attention when the elements that are indeed primary are appropriately cared for.[9]

Gibbs provides a clear definition of what truly is primary to all Christians and churches. He writes,

> Discipleship simply means the imitation of Christ (1 Thessalonians 1:6)...A disciple is one who embodies the message he or she proclaims. It was to people who were themselves disciples that Jesus gave the Great Commission to disciple the nations. The implication is clear—it takes a disciple to make a disciple. We reproduce after our own kind. Undiscipled church members present one of the greatest challenges facing the church, not only in the West but around the world.[10]

To be a true disciple of Christ, to carry out the Great Commission, and to disciple the nations are primary aspects of one's faith. But it is unlikely that Christians will carry out the Great Commission out if fewer than 10 percent of Christians are having a daily intimate personal relationship with Christ. It is impossible to imitate Christ if 90 percent of Christians do not come close to Christ by talking to him, listening to him, and following him.

Two Great Omissions

In his book, *The Great Omission*, Willard actually points out two great omissions to Jesus' Great Commission:

> Having made disciples, these alone were to be baptized into the name of the Father, and of the Son, and of the Holy Spirit. Given this twofold preparation, they were then to be taught to treasure and keep "all things whatsoever I have commanded you" (Matthew 28:20). The Christian church of the first centuries resulted from following this plan for church growth—a result hard to improve upon. But in place of Christ's plan, historical drift has substituted "Make converts and baptize them into church membership." This causes two great omissions from the Great Commission to stand out. Most important, we start by omitting the making of disciples and enrolling people as Christ's students, when we should let all else wait for that. Then we also omit, of necessity, the step of taking our converts through training that will bring them ever-increasingly to do what Jesus directed. These two great omissions are connected in practice into one whole. Not having made our converts disciples, it is impossible for us to teach them how to live as Christ lived and taught (Luke 14:26).[11]

In considering how Christians can become disciples of Christ, it is certainly difficult if they do not even have a daily intimate personal relationship with Christ. Willard explains that there is a serious problem of a "case of the missing teacher." He writes,

> Right at the heart of this alienation lies the absence of Jesus the teacher from our lives. Strangely, we seem prepared to learn how to live from almost anyone but him. We are ready to believe that the "latest studies" have more to teach us about love and sex than he does…The disappearance of Jesus as teacher explains why today in Christian churches—of whatever learning—little effort is made to teach people to do what he did and taught.[12]

It is exactly because of these two great omissions and the "case of the missing teacher" that Christians need to put micro discipleship into practice. The result would be that more and more Christians would become disciples of Christ, "being" Christ in this world so that they truly carry out his Great Commission.

Hearing God

As stated in the Introduction of this paper, micro discipleship is a mentoring discipleship strategy toward Christlikeness based on the first stage of the parable of the seeds in Mark 4:28-29. The missing DNA is in the first stage—the stalk. It is daily devotion—a daily intimate and personal relationship with God through prayers and reading the Bible so that believers can hear God's voice. This is the primary discipleship development that all Christians need to have. And, as Willard states, believers need assistance from those who understand the divine voice from their own experience to lead those who are willing to learn.

> With assistance from those who understand the divine voice from their own experience and with an openness and will to learn on our part, we can come to recognize the voice of God without great difficulty...Without qualified help which works alongside our own desire to learn and readiness to cooperate, God's direct word will most likely remain a riddle or at best a game of theological charades.[13]

In this way, Micro-Macro Discipling needs to be a mentoring discipleship strategy because it is critical to have both disciplers and mentors to help Christians in the process of discipleship development. In my own experience, I was called to be a discipler when I launched two blogs and two podcasts since March 2011. These activities have helped many Christians to establish a workable and enjoyable daily devotion. I spend approximately two hours a day to help my readers and listeners from 113 countries to have a daily intimate personal relationship with God. In total I have spent over four thousands hours to help people hear God so that they can become true disciples of Jesus.

From Discipleship Development to Apostolic Commitment

The process of re-establishing a daily intimate personal relationship with Jesus leads Christians to be true disciples of Christ. Gibbs explains,

> Groups that promote discipleship tend to focus on the personal,

spiritual growth aspects. Their concern is more with the inward journey of faith than the outward venture of communicating that faith in all its dimensions. In contrast to this introspective model, we find in the New Testament that discipleship was linked to apostleship. Learning together from the Lord leads to going out into the world in his name.[14]

The mentoring discipleship strategy of micro discipleship should, as Gibbs states, lead to an outward focus. When the missing DNA of discipleship development—that is, daily devotion—is replaced, it leads to apostolic commitment, which will lead to macro church planting. This is truly living out Jesus' parable of the seeds: beginning with the stalk and ending in the harvest.

Micro Discipleship in the Context of the Incarnation

The idea of Micro-Macro Discipling was birthed from a personal time of listening to the Lord Jesus Christ regarding his direction for me in my new role as a bishop in July 2009. I wrote a letter to the sixteen churches I was about to oversee that reflects the meaning of Micro-Macro Discipling (see Appendix H). The letter reflects a practical theology of the incarnation that the experience of being with Christ led me to receive. God's mandate to me is similar to the one received by the apostles in Acts 6:4, which urged them to prayer and the ministry of the Word. My letter to the churches also reflects the means by which we are called to carry out that mandate: connecting, relationship, and unity.

Connecting

Connecting in this context means the process of a mentor connecting with and leading two to three new disciples of Christ to establish a daily intimate relationship with Jesus Christ. In this process of connecting, the depth of a mentor is increased: he or she starts in the role of a discipler, moves on to becoming an evangelist, then becomes a mentor, and finally becomes a church planter. In these roles, he or she is able to raise up more disciples to be able to take all four mentoring roles into a broader phase of his Kingdom ministry.

The Church desperately needs all kinds of mentors, especially in those four categories. Kimball states that the emerging church must see generations connecting.[15] He stresses the importance of a mentor by sharing how he met three of his mentors in their sixties, eighties, and nineties. He gives an example of Rod Clendenen, one of his mentors who is over eighty years old. Kimball writes, "He teaches, by his life, how important it is not to depend on the church for your Bible intake but to learn to feed yourself from God's Word. These lessons could never have been taught with the same impact they had in sermons or classes. They can be taught only through mentoring, as generations interact with one another outside of a church setting."[16]

When I look at how God used three mentors to help Dan Kimball to be a better disciple of Christ, I think of how God prepared me for my role as a bishop through six mentors, long before I became a bishop. Without the mentoring of John Stott in 1991 and for many years afterwards, I would have been a self-centered, self-seeking Anglican priest without connecting personally with Christ and unwilling to submit to the Lordship of Christ. I would not have learned the importance of Christlikeness, and I would not have been able to receive this micro discipleship strategic plan. Without the mentoring of Dr. Gil Stieglitz since 2005, I would not be in the DMin program at Fuller and might be another burned-out pastor. Without the sponsorship of Dr. S. K. Lee, I would not have been able to enroll in the DMin program. Without the mentoring of Bishop Thomas Johnston and Archbishop Ping Chung Yong during the past six years, I would not have become a bishop. Without the mentoring of Professor Terry Walling, I would not have a clear vision of this Micro-Macro Discipleship strategic plan. All these mentoring opportunities have allowed me to connect in one way or another, and have encouraged me to focus on God's Kingdom plan working through me in Canada and beyond.

Relationships

Relationships in this context refers to the willingness of more individuals to become disciplers, evangelists, mentors, and church planters. For each of these four roles, the goal ought to be successfully leading disciples of Christ to acquire a simple, focused, and deep way of having a daily intimate relationship with Jesus, and to enjoy that relationship daily. With the building up of this primary relationship with Christ and the willingness to listen and obey to the lordship of Christ, all relationships involved will be enriched and strengthened.

In his book, *The Jesus Creed*, Scott McKnight asserts that the goal of a disciple of Jesus is relationship, not perfection.[17] Stanley and Clinton provide a clear picture of the importance of mentoring and how believers can achieve mentoring relationships that build up bridges rather than destroy bridges.[18] Micro-Macro Discipling builds bridges related to one's relationship with God, one's relationship with other Christians, and one's relationship with other non-believers through all kinds of godly relationships. The idea of raising up disciplers, evangelists, mentors, and church planters in the four-year strategic plan is to increase and enhance a deeper relationship with God, both with those in the Church and with those not yet in the kingdom.

Robert Logan also emphasizes the importance of relationships in his book, *Beyond Church Planting*:

> Everything in the kingdom of God is about relationship—loving God and loving others. Relationship is the vehicle that God uses to bring redemption. It is at the core of community and the very fabric of the Christian life. The Church functions in the context of three relationships: our relationship with God, our relationship with those in the Church, and our relationship with those not yet in the kingdom.[19]

The key word related to being in his Kingdom is "relationship." In their book, *Churches That Multiply*, Elmer Towns and Douglas Porter state that Christianity is more than doctrine: it is relational.[20] They contend that at the very core of a believer's faith is the belief that God wants a relationship with each individual. Randy Frazee, in *The Connecting Church*, offers a different perspective by stating that "isolation" is the second obstacle to connecting a person into relationships and into a true community.[21] He explains that the contemporary human condition flows out of the first major obstacle, namely, a culture of individualism, which promises to give the best but only to inflict the disease of loneliness. Through building "relationships," the obstacles of "isolation" and "individualism" will not be able to pull people away from his Kingdom. It is in micro discipleship that the relationship God most wants to establish in our lives can be firmly grounded.

Unity

The process of connecting and building up relationships leads to unity, as described by Jesus in John 17:20-23:

> My prayer is not for them alone. I pray also for those who will believe in me through their message, that all of them may be one, Father, just as you are in me and I am in you. May they also be in us so that the

world may believe that you have sent me. I have given them the glory that you gave me, that they may be one as we are one—I in them and you in me—so that they may be brought to complete unity. Then the world know that you sent me and have loved them even as you have loved me. (NIV)

In the summer of 1992, I was leading a group of twenty-four clergy and youth leaders from the Anglican Church of Hong Kong to participate in a one-week course on evangelism, under Professor John Stott in his school of evangelism in London. During the course, Stott told the group that the most important chapter in the Bible is John 17. Stott's reason for this claim was that John 17 is Jesus' last word of teaching to his apostles, and that these words contained the essence of Jesus' final direction for them. Jesus told them to be one as he was one with the Father. Jesus' prayer was that his disciples be brought to complete unity with him and with the Father. With this in mind, incarnation is connecting to the relationships God has for his people, particularly the daily intimate personal relationship with himself, so that believers may taste the sweetness of unity that is so lacking in today's Church.

---

[1] Willard, *The Spirit of the Disciplines*, 14.

[2] Dan Kimball, *The Emerging Church* (Grand Rapids: Zondervan, 2003), 79.

[3] Stott, *The Radical Disciple*, 31, 35.

[4] Thomas Torrance, *Incarnation: The Person and Life of Christ* (Downers Grove, IL: InterVarsity Press, 2008), 2.

[5] Michael Frost and Alan Hirsch, *The Shaping of Things to Come* (Peabody, MA: Hendrickson, 2003), 12.

[6] Ibid., 42.

[7] Ibid., 13.

[8] Ibid., 36-37.

[9] Dallas Willard, *Renovation of the Heart* (Colorado Springs: NavPress, 2002), 235-36.

[10] Eddie Gibbs, *Church Next* (Downers Grove IL: InterVarsity, 2000), 230-31.

[11] Dallas Willard, *The Great Omission* (New York: Harper SanFrancisco, 2006), 5-6.

[12] Dallas Willard, *The Divine Conspiracy* (New York: Harper One, 1997), 55-57.

[13] Dallas Willard, *Hearing God* (Downers Grove, IL: InterVarsity Press, 1999), 169.

[14] Gibbs, *Church Next*, 233.

[15] Kimball, *The Emerging Church*, 218.

[16] Ibid., 219.

[17] Scott McKnight, *The Jesus Creed* (Orleans, MA: Paraclete, 2004), 183.

[18] Stanley and Clinton, *Connecting*.

[19] Robert E. Logan, *Beyond Church Planting* (St. Charles, IL: ChurchSmart, 2005), 22.

[20] Elmer Towns and Douglas Porter, *Churches That Multiply* (Kansas City, MO: Beacon Hill, 2003), 112.

[21] Randy Frazee, *The Connecting Church* (Grand Rapids: Zondervan, 2001).

PART THREE

STRATEGY

CHAPTER SEVEN

DISCIPLING STAGE

Roland Allen provides a clear picture of how important it was for St. Paul to have a strategy, and how that strategy became the source of the overflowing streams to all parts of the whole world. Allen writes, "St. Paul seized strategic points because he had a strategy. The foundation of churches in them was part of a campaign. In his hands they became the sources of rivers, mints from which the new coin of the Gospel was spread in every direction."[1] Chapters 7 and 8 present a strategy for churches and Christians in a similar dynamic and with similar momentum. It is hoped that this simple, deep, and focused strategy will become the source of mints from which not only the new coin but the old and original coin of the Gospel will spread in every direction.

The strategic plan is a four-year plan divided into two parts. The first part consists of a two-year "discipling stage," during which disciples and evangelists will be raised up. This is a two-year plan to help more Christians to become disciples and evangelists so that they can help two to three Christians to become disciples and evangelists. The second part, which is presented in Chapter 8, consists of a two-year "mentoring stage," during which mentors and church planters will be raised up.

Reggie McNeal gives a true picture of the need to have a plan in teaching, preparing, and raising leaders. He writes, "Unfortunately, spiritual leaders often resist developing teams around them. This malpractice results in heart blockages and heart damage. Their failure to develop community contributes to the heart diseases of loneliness, feelings of insignificance, and spiritual and emotional debilitation that accompany isolation."[2] As McNeal describes, truly loneliness and isolation are the cause of burnout for quite a number of Christian leaders. The need to develop teams is a key to the micro discipleship strategy. Such a focus upon building up leadership teams would surely lessen the chances of having more leaders fall into the pits of loneliness and isolation.

David Garrison, in his book, *Church Planting Movements*, states the reason why most churches do not have any church plants:

> Without a common vision, they will cast off restraint and the people they are trying to reach will perish. Missionary leaders are learning

that they must clearly state and restate the vision for a Church Planting Movement...If we don't really believe that a Church Planting Movement is possible, we won't take the actions needed to usher it into existence. Church Planting Movement practitioners come to believe, see, feel, and taste the movement well before it dawns into reality.[3]

The Church desperately needs a vision from Jesus Christ our Lord to further his Kingdom growth. This is true not only in regards to church planting, which is a macro plan, but also for Micro-Macro discipling, believers' basic daily intimate relationship with Christ. If churches can live out the micro plan, then the macro growth will come naturally. Jesus says, "This is what the kingdom of God is like. A man scatters seed on the ground. Night and day, whether he sleeps or gets up, the seed sprouts and grows, though he does not know how. All by itself the soil produces grain—first the stalk, then the head, the full kernel in the head. As soon as the grain is ripe, he puts the sickle to it, because the harvest has come" (Mark 4:26-29). The job of Christian leaders, as described in previous chapters, is to prepare the soil so that at least the stalk comes out. The most difficult part of farming and gardening is this beginning, the "micro" part. Once this phase is secured, then the other three stages will come with lesser effort. Christian leaders need a clear and simple vision, executed to perfection, so that Jesus' parable of the sower (Mark 4:1-20) and parable of the growing seed (Mark 4:26-29) take place. In so doing, disciples of Christ will be fruitful and will multiply, obeying Jesus' command.

The strategy of Micro-Macro Discipling is a leadership farm system. Lay Christians are being trained to be farmers and gardeners, following Jesus' parable of the growing seeds model. Logan writes, "The idea of leadership farm systems is not new. It is an older and more prolific model for training than today's prevalent classroom/curriculum model. The mentoring process is much like the Hebrew model of instruction."[4] Logan continues by outlining the reason, goal, and content of a leadership farm system: "Leadership farm systems seek to bring people into the fullest possible extent of what God has uniquely gifted them to become. The church is structured so that no matter where a growing Christian is on the spectrum of leadership development, there is a place for them and they are challenged to take the next step in their own spiritual growth and development."[5]

Logan's farm system echoes Cole's idea that a church multiplication movement should be developed like a cell, which eventually multiplies and morphs into more complex living entities.[6] The four-year plan of Anglican Mission Canada and beyond is from micro discipleship to macro church planting, according to the idea of Jesus' parable of the growing seeds in Mark 4. The strategies must be simple, focused, and deep in their impact. The four components of the strategies are: 1) Discipling: connecting people to God and each other to create a relational climate for raising up disciplers and disciples; 2) Evangelizing: initiating a culture where disciplers and disciples become missional in both lifestyle and practice;[7] 3) Mentoring: providing a mentoring and coaching culture for clergy and leaders to equip and empower the laity for missional ministry and greater impact in God's Kingdom work, as well as to raise up more mentors and coaches to extend his Kingdom; and 4) Planting: raising up more church planters and new congregations that emerge out of the previous three years of raising up disciplers, evangelists, and mentors.

The Importance of a Discipler

In 1 Corinthians 3:9, Paul writes, "For we are God's fellow workers; you are God's field, God's building." Paul tells believers here that they are farmers and fellow workers of Christ who are meant to work in the field with Christ. Jesus also discusses the work of believers and his provision of rest in the midst of work: "Come to me, all who labor and are heavy laden, and I will give you rest. Take my yoke upon you, and learn from me, for I am gentle and lowly in heart, and you will find rest for your souls. For my yoke is easy, and my burden is light" (Matthew 11:28-30). When Jesus mentions taking his yoke, the listener imagines two cows working in the field, bearing the same yoke on their necks. Jesus tells us to learn from him in this way so that we who labor and are heavy laden can rest and not burn out. So many Christians burn out because they do not have this kind of relationship with Christ. It is a discipler's job to take up the yoke and help a disciple of Christ to work in the field as his fellow worker, thus learning Christlikeness.

Stott writes, "Christlikeness is the purpose of God for the people of God."[8] Since the day of my visit with John Stott in 2009, during which he impressed upon me the importance of Christlikeness, the goal of Christlikeness has been like a seal imprinted in my heart as the sole purpose of my life. The strategy of micro discipleship involves one discipler helping two or three disciples of Christ to enjoy a daily intimate personal relationship with Jesus, and to live out a lifestyle of Christlikeness. It is a discipler's job to help disciples of Christ to experience that Christ is their fellow worker, tending the field with them and helping them to be transformed into true disciples of Christ.

Historically speaking, there are ample examples of how disciplers raised up powerful disciples. In the Old Testament, Moses famously raised up Joshua, and Elijah famously raised up Elisha. Chapter 4 discusses the discipleship of John and Andrew by John the Baptist; Peter, James, and John by Jesus; Paul and John Mark by Barnabas; and Silas, Timothy, and Titus by Paul. Without following Jesus' and Paul's examples of raising up disciplers, the Church would not have extended so widely in such a short period of time.

It is a critical situation, then, that the raising up of disciplers has not been a focus for most churches in today's Church. New Christians are usually invited to some kind of newcomers' class or baptism class, and then put into fellowship or small groups. Due to the lack of a one-on-one or one-on-two level of follow-up by a discipler, most Christians miss the golden opportunity in their early stage, the micro stage, to form the habit of having a daily intimate personal relationship with Jesus. Skipping this level is like missing the first stage of farming: by not having healthy growth during the stalk stage, it is very difficult for the seed to grow into a full kernel or to reach the time of harvest. For this reason, many churches are stuck, especially in North America. The fact that fewer than 10 percent of Christians are having daily devotion is directly due to the fact that new Christians are not being properly discipled.

Personal Example of Discipling Two Young Teens

It is not easy to encourage Christians to be disciples. To help more people to know that this model of being a discipler works, I put myself on a test to be a discipler for two teens, Athanasius, our younger son, and Vance, his best friend. I began on January 1, 2009 and completed the official discipleship phase in August 31, 2011. The total amount of time involved was two years and eight months. It was important for me to have this experience so that I may lead by proven examples. The experience was difficult at times, but eventually rewarding.[9]

At the end of the official discipleship phase, these two teens understood how to have a daily intimate relationship with Jesus; they knew how to listen to Jesus' voice and how to write down what Jesus told them in their spiritual journals. Athanasius and Vance have now become two young leaders serving in our church. They have started to share their faith with their classmates and successfully brought a few of them to our English worship and the teens' small group. This is quite a change from the time before I started this long period of discipling, when they were disconnected from Jesus and from the Church. They had to go to Sunday school because of their parents, but they did not enjoy it. I am quite sure that if not for this very special opportunity for me to walk with Athan and Vance for such a long period of time, they would have left the Church and would have no relationship with Jesus now. This is a vivid example of how I used the micro part of Micro-Macro Discipling in an effective way.

Personal Example of Teaching a Master of Ministry Course at a Megachurch of Five Thousand People

We have discussed the results of a survey completed by approximately three hundred leaders and members of a mega church in which I taught a Master of Ministry course in winter 2009. My experience teaching that course provided me with information regarding a devastating situation in discipleship development. During the course, I presented the eight types of mentoring from Stanley and Clinton's book, *Connecting*, in order to explain the importance of various type of mentoring.[10] I asked the students to write down the numbers of helpful mentors they had been in relationship with since they had become Christians, according to the eight types of mentors. The results were striking in that they had had very few mentoring relationships, especially disciplers. The class was comprised of twenty-five students, all of whom were pastors and regional directors of this megachurch, which has more than two hundred small groups.

Discipler	**12**
Spiritual Guide	**91**
Coach	**37**
Counselor	**39**
Teacher	**280**
Sponsor	**51**
Contemporary	**176**
Historical	**108**

Figure 1. Number of Various Mentors for Twenty-Five Pastors and Leaders in a Megachurch (2009)

Most of them were in tears when they suddenly realized that their personal spiritual growth struggles were due to a lack of disciplers in the "micro" stage of their development. This reality also brought them to a new awareness that the main reason why so many Christians (including themselves and their small group members) do not have daily devotion is because they did not have disciplers to walk with them during the early stages of their faith.

Personal Example of a New Church Plant in a Chinese Seafood Restaurant Using the Discipler 123 Model[11]

To further test the Micro-Macro Discipleship theory, I launched a new bishop's pioneer ministry in March 2011: a new church plant in a Chinese seafood restaurant. I received this vision the winter of 2010 and talked to one of our parishioners, Tony Wong, whom I had baptized together with his wife, his son, his daughter-in-law, and his two grandchildren. Tony is the owner of three big Chinese seafood restaurants in our area, Richmond, British Columbia. I worked with a Baptist pastor and started an Alpha course in one of Tony's three restaurants in March. So far, I have baptized ten restaurant workers.

The name of this new church plant is Emmanuel 330. The "330" is in reference to the worshipping time, which is 3:30 p.m. This first church plant is having its worship at 3:30 p.m. every Wednesday. Most of the Chinese restaurants finish their business around 3:00 p.m. every day and then start again at 5:30 p.m. During this two and a half hour break, quite a number of restaurant workers go to gamble in casinos or take naps in their cars or a corner of the restaurant. I intentionally chose this strategic time and invited a Baptist pastor and four leaders from my church, Richmond Emmanuel Church, to put Discipler 123 to the test. The church plant launch team sent out flyers in the area, and about twelve people came to the Alpha course, which preceded the official church plant, taking place between March and June.

Each Wednesday the daily passage in my Discipler 123 blog and podcast (both in English and Chinese) was used as the daily reading. After listening to my reading of that passage through the podcast, there was a time of sharing to discuss what they heard from Jesus, and then a Bible study on the passage. Then the recording of my sharing in the daily podcast was played, and we had a time of prayer in groups of three or four. Most importantly, the members of the group were encouraged to have daily devotion using my blog and podcast. Most of the people are now having daily devotion, and a core group of faithful disciples of

Christ has been formed. It is hoped that each member of this new church plant will be able to have a daily intimate personal relationship with Jesus and be willing to be a discipler, an evangelist, a mentor, and a church planter.

The Role of a Discipler

The role of a discipler is significant, both for his or her disciple as well as for the Church as a whole. Disciplers should be characterized by several qualities: having a Kingdom view, having a heart like Jesus' heart, and having the lifestyle of an apostle. Each of these qualities contributes to the success of a good discipler.

Kingdom View

A discipler needs to be able to bring a kingdom view and a kingdom value to his or her apprentices. It is the role of the discipler to impress upon his or her apprentices that they are in the body of Christ and under Kingdom authority, not in a "club," enjoying inner-circle privileges. Mc Neal writes, "Kingdom thinking challenges church thinking. Kingdom thinking does not force people into the church to hear about Jesus or maintain that church membership is the same thing as kingdom citizenship…Kingdom vision requires kingdom values to support it…The clash between club member values and missionary values has claimed a lot of casualties."[12] A discipler should be able to teach his or her apprentices not to spend time on church growth but rather on kingdom growth.

Jesus' Heart

McNeal offers three good reflections regarding how to acquire Jesus' heart in a simple and practical way. The first is to say "thank you" to one's "Jethro" and to have the willingness to become a Jethro.[13] To be a discipler is to follow Moses' example of having a discipler himself, who was Moses' father-in-law, Jethro, and to be willing to become a discipler, a "Jethro." The role of a discipler is to naturally transition to a deeper relational role as a mentor.

McNeal's second idea related to having Jesus' heart is to re-examine the call and to head towards his Kingdom agenda. Jesus' heart is to remind his disciples of their calling and to inspire them that they are being caught up in something bigger than they are so that they might focus on his Kingdom agenda. Disciplers should be in line with Jesus' heart so that they can be used by Jesus for his strategic purposes.[14]

McNeal's third idea related to having Jesus' heart is to wait for the Lord and to rest in the Lord. So many Christians are unintentionally overscheduled with programs and classes, and are constantly bombarded by emails and phone calls. A discipler with Jesus' heart should be able to lead by example, waiting upon the Lord and taking time for the Sabbath.[15]

Gene Wilkes, in his book, *Jesus on Leadership*, also provides a good example of what it means to have Jesus' heart to lead.[16] He discusses Jesus' personal example of leadership. There are three qualities of Jesus' heart that should characterize a leader: servant leadership, a focus on building disciples rather than "warehouse Christians," and a focus on equipping others for service and building a team.

First of all, a leader should be a servant. Wilkes states clearly what a discipler should do to raise up disciples of Christ: "The leader becomes servant to those who have joined him when he provides adequate vision, direction, correction, and resources to carry out the mission entrusted to the group. The leader serves when he equips others and 'teams' with them to reach the goal of mission together. Leadership begins when a God-revealed mission captures a person."[17] A discipler must receive a kingdom order from the King to become a servant leader.

Second, Wilkes challenges disciplers regarding whether they are building a warehouse or a factory.[18] In fact, contends Wilkes, many churches and Christians are building warehouses—where believers gather—but not factories—where believers multiply. A discipler's vision should be to build a factory to produce more disciples of Christ and to release them to do his Kingdom work.

Third, Wilkes states that leaders should focus on equipping others for service and building real teams.[19] He details five steps that should be taken for equipping others for service: encourage them to serve, qualify them to serve, understand their needs, instruct them, and pray for them. He also presents four steps for building real teams: create a sense of togetherness, empower with authority and presence, account for the mission and the team's actions, and be a mentor.

Apostle's Lifestyle

A discipler must also have the lifestyle of an apostle in order to be successful. Acts 6:4 states very clearly what apostle's lifestyle looks like: "We will give our attention to prayer and the ministry of the word." In his book, *Deepening Your Conversation with God*, Ben Petterson writes, "Our souls are like that well [of living water]. If we do not draw on the living water that Jesus promised would well up in us like a spring, our hearts close and dry up…The consequence for not drinking deeply of God is to eventually lose the ability to drink at all. Prayerlessness is its own punishment, both its disease and its cause. That's the deeper meaning to our fatigue in the ministry."[20] A discipler's role is also an apostle's role: to teach people to pray and to be in the ministry of God's Word. Prayerlessness and being without daily devotion is the lifestyle of this present age. The challenge for every discipler is to turn that around, and to raise up disciples of Christ who have a daily intimate personal relationship with Jesus.

---

[1] Roland Allen, *Missionary Methods: St. Paul's or Ours?* (Grand Rapids: Eerdmans Publishing, 1962), 17.

[2] Reggie McNeal, *A Work of the Heart* (San Francisco: Jossey-Bass Publishers, 2000), 133.

[3] David Garrison, *Church Planting Movements* (Bangalore, India: WIGTake Resources, 2004), 240-41.

[4] Robert E. Logan, "Biblical & Historical Examples of Leadership Farm System," from Coachnet, an online teaching website available to students in Logan's classes.

[5] Robert E. Logan, "The Goals of a Leadership Farm System," from Coachnet, an online teaching website available to students in Logan's classes.

[6] Cole, *Organic Church*, 24.

[7] *Missional* means that all of them are conscious of leading non-Christian relatives and friends to know Jesus and receive him as Saviour and Lord of life.

[8] Stott, *The Radical Disciple*, 31.

[9] Appendix I contains a daily entry from my blog on October 24, 2009, forty weeks after I began the discipleship process.

[10] Stanley and Clinton, *Connecting*, 41.

[11] Discipler 123, as described in Chapter 1 of this paper, is the ACiC's first-year campaign to create momentum for launching the micro discipleship movement. The campaign invites members of ACiC churches to become disciplers and to spend three months helping two new Christians to have daily devotion with the help of my blogs as a devotional tool.

[12] McNeal, *The Present Future*, 34, 102.

[13] Ibid., 10.

[14] Ibid., 98-99.

[15] Ibid., 138-47.

[16] Gene Wilkes, *Jesus on Leadership* (Wheaton, IL: Tyndale, 1999).

[17] Ibid., 18-19.

[18] Ibid., 102.

[19] Ibid., 189, 238.

[20] Ben Petterson, *Deepening Your Conversation with God* (Minneapolis: Bethany House, 1999), 43-44.

CHAPTER EIGHT

MENTORING STAGE

This chapter focuses on the second phase: developing mentors and church planters. The importance of a mentor is discussed, followed by sections on understanding mentoring, the stages of mentoring, and the role of a mentor.

The Importance of a Mentor

There are several reasons why the mentoring role is so important. These reasons include: 1) to provide spiritual formation; 2) to help with changes and transitions; 3) to help believers finish well; and 4) to raise up church planters. Each of these activities on the part of the mentor benefits the one being mentored as well as the entire Church.

To Provide Spiritual Formation

The return to spiritual formation is such an important call for the Church. McNeal names the need to utilize mentors in the process of spiritual formation. He writes, "This means that helping people develop emotionally, physically, and relationally is all spiritual...I am recommending that churches provide life coaching for people. We need to view this as spiritual formation."[1] Indeed, mentoring is desperately needed in the process of spiritual formation just as teachers are needed in the process of education. The role of teachers should not only involve teaching their students but should include helping them to develop emotionally, physically, and relationally.

To Help with Changes and Transitions

William Bridges, in his book, *Transitions*, offers a new paradigm to explain the difference between change and transition: "One of the most important differences between a change and a transition is that changes are driven to reach a goal, but transitions start with letting go of what no longer fits or is adequate to the life stage you are in. You need to figure out for yourself what exactly that no-longer-appropriate thing is."[2] For this reason, mentors are needed to help leaders to make such important discernment. Clinton and Stanley state that the important job of mentors is to connect them to the core of discipleship.[3] Without a mentor, Christians may be wandering around in various directions and places, unable to find a purpose. Just as Edwin Friedman writes in his book, *A Failure of Nerve,* "Contemporary American civilization is as misoriented about the environment of relationships as the medieval world was misoriented about the Earth and the sky."[4]

Helping people move from misoriented to reorienting marks the importance of a mentor. It is in this kind of mentoring relationship that Christians can have a better understanding of themselves and their whereabouts. The discipling stage ought to lead people in their early stages as Christians so that they can have a daily intimate personal relationship with Jesus through daily devotion, and so that they will be willing to lead their relatives and friends to Jesus as disciplers and evangelists. This mentoring stage ought to lead people into Christian maturity so that they will have a deeper spiritual life, comprised of reading spiritual books and taking courses, and so that they will be willing to join in church serving and planting teams.

To Help with Finishing Well

Bob Buford, in his book, *Finishing Well,* states very clearly that if believers want to finish well, they need to find their core personality, that is, who they really are. He writes, "Once you accept the idea that you want the second half of your life to major on significance, the next step is to focus on finding the core of your personality—the immovable center of who you really are."[5] Buford then quotes Peter Drucker, who states that finding who one really is and making important life changes is to "reposition" oneself for a new role.[6]

Finishing well is perhaps one of the most important goals for a leader to look forward to, but it is not easy to attain unless that leader has a good mentor. According to significant research, one out of three leaders does not finish well.[7] Dan Allender, in his book, *Leading with a Limp,* discusses the options for effective solutions when facing the five primary leadership challenges: crisis, complexity, betrayal, loneliness, and weariness. He states that the solutions are to change from cowardice, rigidity, narcissism, hiding, and fatalism to courage, depth, gratitude, openness, and hope.[8] Knowing the complexity of the ineffective responses provides a glimpse into the reality that finishing well is not easy. Allender's concept strikes a chord for me personally in that there have been times when I did not know how to pull myself out of those ineffective responses. The five challenges of leadership are a reality, and leaders are unable to finish well unless they have mentors helping them to learn to open themselves up to the effective responses.

In his book, *Stuck! Navigating Life and Leadership Transitions*, Walling devotes three chapters to mentoring, and titles them "Awakening," "Deciding," and "Finishing."[9] Walling asserts that mentors are to help disciples so that they might have a personal awakening in order to discern a call from God, to decide on what is their major role, and to avoid wasting time on non-essential activities so that they can finish well. These three stages are not difficult to understand, but they are difficult to carry out. Many people get stuck, and at these times mentors are needed to help people go through various major transitions. Walling states, "Your development will move you from one stage to another. The word 'development' means 'the unfolding.'"[10] Believers need to have mentors so that they might understand how much they need to allow God to unfold different chapters of their lives so that they can go through the three stages of awakening, deciding, and finishing well.

To Raise Up Church Planters

On October 18, 2007, an article was written in *Christianity Today* regarding the self-proclaimed failures of Willow Creek Community Church (hereafter, Willow Creek) in Chicago.[11] Bill Hybels, senior pastor of the church, confessed that the church had made a mistake. This confession came after Willow Creek released findings from a multiple-year qualitative study of its ministry. The results were published in a book titled, *Reveal: Where Are You?* co-authored by Greg Hawkins, executive pastor of Willow Creek. Hybels called the findings "earth shaking," "ground breaking," and "mind blowing." Hybels stated, "We made a mistake. What we should have done when people crossed the line of faith and become Christians, we should have started telling people and teaching people that they have to take responsibility to become 'self feeders.' We should have gotten people, taught people, how to read their Bible between service, how to do the spiritual practices much more aggressively on their own."[12]

Ed Stetzer and David Putman, in their book, *Breaking the Missional Code*, clearly illustrate the pitfall of megachurch model:

So while many pastors have struggled with "doing church" in their contexts, successful pastors have discovered God's unique vision for their local churches, often learning from others. They became missional churches where God had placed them. They broke the missional code in their own neighbourhoods instead of applying proven strategies of innovative pastors around the country, instead of focusing on church growth or church health gurus.[13]

In the trend of so many "copy and paste" models from successful stories of megachurches, many churches are feeling stuck. There are not many like Bill Hybels and Rick Warren in this world to build their megachurches. But there are numerous faithful pastors who are ready to build and plant churches according to God's tailor-made plans for their specific churches. Mentors are critical in that they can help individual believers to become missional people, and the churches to which they belong to become missional churches. As such, they will no longer simply be "doing church," but instead they will be multiplying and birthing churches according to Jesus' Great Commission. A mentor's responsibility is to raise up mature and faithful disciples of Christ and church planters to extend God's Kingdom.

Logan asserts that church multiplication movements can happen anywhere, at any time.[14] He discusses John Wesley, and how in his lifetime saw 72,000 people in England and 57,000 people in the United States become followers of Christ. In the generation after his death, at one point, one in every thirty adults in England was a Methodist. Wesley's secret was a simple, reproducible method—a system that empowered ordinary people to do extraordinary things.[15]

Logan offers other vivid examples of churches that grow and multiply rapidly. One such church is New Life Fellowship in Bombay, India. Founded in 1968, by 1980 the church had only about one hundred members. After emphasizing church multiplication, as of 2000 there were approximately twelve hundred house churches in 250 worship centers with an estimated attendance of 50,000. Most of the churches are still renting their worship places and offices. Another example is Awakening Chapel, founded in 1998 by Neil Cole, author of *Organic Church*. Today there are at least 375 organic churches that are part of this movement, which spread over twelve countries in less than four years.[16]

Garrison reports that there are 30,000 people baptized every day now in China, and he gives many examples of the immense growth of church multiplication. In Africa, one Muslim boy experienced God and later founded a church in the 1990s. Out of this one church, by 2000 there were four thousand churches, within which 150,000 people had received Christ. In northern India, there were only twenty-eight churches in the 1980s. By the 1990s there were 1,720 churches, within which 55,000 people were baptized, and by 2000, there were 5,400 churches, within which 83,000 people were baptized.[17] Logan writes, "Success from a Christian perspective is simply to 'find out what God wants you to do...and do it.'...Effective leaders take time to cultivate vision from God and to help others embrace the vision as their own."[18]

George Patterson and Richard Scoggins, in their book, *Church Multiplication Guide*, state that a reproducing church needs a firm vision that it belongs to the living, reproducing body of Christ and therefore receives from God all that it needs to reproduce.[19] Jesus says, "The harvest is plentiful but the workers are few" (Matthew 9: 37). Only Jesus can see that the harvest is plentiful and coming. A church needs a vision from God that it can see through God's eyes.

In his book, *The Forgotten Ways*, Alan Hirsch recalls experience at a seminar on missional church during which the participants were asked to ponder how the early Church could grow from 25,000 Christians in AD 100 to twenty million Christians in AD 310.[20] The speaker's question haunted him: "How did they do this? How did they grow from being a small movement to the most significant religious force in the Roman Empire in two centuries?"[21] Hirsch's answer is what he calls Apostolic Genius with the missional DNA. At the centre of his Apostolic Genius is the fact that Jesus is Lord, and from that truth are generated his five elements: "Disciple Making," "Missional-Incarnational Impulse," "Apostolic Environment," "Organic Systems," and "Communitas, not Community."[22] Truly, the members of the early Church received a vision from the Lord Jesus Christ. They "saw" the tailor-made strategy for having Christians discipled and churches multiplied.

Garrison writes, "A Church Planting Movement is a rapid multiplication of indigenous churches planting churches that sweeps through a people group or population segment."[23] It was beyond human effort that the early Church could grow as rapidly as it did. Without a vision from Jesus as King and Lord, church multiplication is impossible. For this reason, many churches are dying or experiencing plateau; they are unable to receive any vision from Christ and are simply striving with human endeavor.

All of these churches that grew and multiplied—the early Church, St. Patrick's movement, Wesley's churches, and the Church in China today, among others—received a vision from Jesus as their Lord. Even in the business field, Starbucks and Wal-Mart have experienced this type of growth, and each of these companies started with a vision. Joseph Michelli, in his book, *The Starbucks Experience*, states clearly that Starbucks started with a vision from its chairman, Howard Schultz. He states, "A vision and a plan executed to perfection are what characterize great businesses."[24] If Starbucks can open five new stores every day, one wonders why the Church cannot experience a similar growth rate.[25] It is certainly possible, as is evident in the examples presented here. For these churches, their success lies in the fact that each one has received a vision from Jesus Christ who is their Lord and King. Thus, mentors are needed desperately to raise up church planters so that Jesus' Great Commission can be accomplished.

Understanding Mentoring

Stanley and Clinton state clearly that mentoring is a relational process:

Mentoring is a relational process in which a mentor, who knows or has experienced something, transfers that something (resources of wisdom, information, experience, confidence, insight, relationships, status, etc.) to a mentoree, at an appropriate time and manner, so that it facilitates development or empowerment.

It takes commitment to build a mentoring relationship, to allow our lives to be teachable and responsive, and to be willing to be held accountable for our growth. But the resulting empowerment and enrichment to our lives are beyond measure.[26]

In order to understand how mentoring differs from discipling, it is important to understand the different types and functions of mentoring. Stanley and Clinton provide a helpful summary of the various mentoring and discipleship roles.[27] There are three types of mentors: intensive, occasional, and passive.

Within the umbrella of "intensive" types of mentors are disciplers, spiritual guides, and coaches. A discipler enables Christians in the basics of following Christ. In the strategy presented in this book, the first two-year stage is focused upon raising disciples. One of the basic responsibilities of a discipler is to raise up disciples and evangelists for Christ so that Christians in their early stages can have an intimate relationship with Christ and start to lead others to Christ. A spiritual guide helps an individual to find accountability, direction, and insight for questions, commitments, and decisions affecting spirituality and maturity. Finally, a coach helps an individual to build up motivation, skill, and application needed to meet a task or a challenge.

There are also three "occasional" types of mentors: a counselor, a teacher, and a sponsor. A counselor gives timely advice and correct perspectives on viewing oneself, others, circumstances, and ministry. A teacher provides knowledge and understanding of a particular subject. And a sponsor provides career guidance and protection as a leader moves within an organization.

There are two "passive" types of mentors: a contemporary model and a historical model. A contemporary model is a living, personal model for one's life, ministry, or profession. This person is not only an example but also inspires emulation. A historical model is someone who is no longer living whose life teaches dynamic principles and values for life, ministry, and/or profession.

These three types and eight functions of mentoring provide a better understanding regarding the difference between the discipling stage and the mentoring stage. The discipling stage consists primarily of the first function among these eight functions. The discipler in this role nurtures new Christians to become true disciples of Christ. The mentoring stage moves on to the other seven functions. Each of these seven uses mentoring deeper-level training of Christians to be mature leaders.

Stages of Mentoring

The four-year plan in understanding the stages of mentoring is according to Jesus' parable of the growing seed in two stages and four types. The first stage is the discipling stage: the micro plan, and the second stage is the mentoring stage: the macro plan. Together these two stages bring about the development of the stalk, the head, the full kernel in the head, and the harvest.

Within the discipling stage is the development of the stalk as well as the head. During the first year, disciplers help new Christians to have a daily intimate personal relationship with Jesus through true daily devotion (the stalk) and to be equipped and prepared to be disciplers themselves. In the second year, one essential feature is added in that those being disciples are now also trained to be evangelists (the head). The focus of the first two years is to have a daily intimate personal relationship with Christ in order to be ready as disciplers and evengelists.

Within the mentoring stage is the development of the full kernel in the head as well as the harvest. During the third year, which is part of the macro movement, those who have been disciplers will be trained to work on a deeper level as mentors. Mentors will equip the new disciplers and evangelists to become mature Christians (the full kernel). In the fourth year, these mature Christians will be mentored to become church planters (the harvest) to plant more groups or churches.

The Role of a Mentor

The importance of a mentor was presented in the first section of this chapter, and those points of importance overlap with the role of a mentor. These points include: 1) to provide spiritual formation; 2) to help with changes and transitions; 3) to help believers finish well; and 4) to raise up church planters. In addition to these four goals, three additional main points regarding the role of a mentor are: connecting, relationships, and unity.

The first role of a mentor is to connect people together in various aspects using various ways. Disconnecting is what has been happening to many Christians all over the world—disconnecting and isolating from relationship with God and with each other, and disconnecting with all kinds of contact points through which people can receive resources and training. It is the role of a mentor to connect everything again according to God's plan, helping people to enter into God's preparations and raising up disciples, evangelists, mentors, and church planters.

The second role of a mentor is through connecting to build up deep and wide relationships with God and others through various basic Christian disciplines and spiritual formation. To put on a program is not difficult, but to build up relationships requires a great deal of time and effort. It is the role of a mentor to lead by example and by building good relationships in all areas so that more Christians can become disciples, evangelists, mentors, and planters.

The third role of a mentor is to build unity in the Church. Jesus stressed the importance of unity in John 17, his last sermon before he was crucified. Jesus knew very well that Satan's main tactic was to destroy the unity of his apostles and disciples. There are so many dissensions in churches which cause people to mistrust the Church and Christians in general. It is the role of a mentor to connect people together, build up genuine relationships, and bring unity to the Church.

On a final note, Cole points out the importance of spending time with people who are "good soil." He writes,

> If ten people accept the Gospel and only two bear fruit, I no longer babysit the unfruitful eight. Instead, I invest my life in the two. These two will bear much fruit. I am convinced that we have made a serious mistake by accommodating bad soil in our churches...We must invest everything in the few who will bear fruit. Life is too short and the potential yields are too great to spend our lives babysitting fruitless people.[28]

Leaders spend too much time with those who are unteachable and un-fruitful. It is imperative that leaders spend their time to teach those who are willing to learn and to be taught.

---

[1] McNeal, *The Present Future*, 75, 77.

[2] William Bridges, *Transitions: Making Sense of Life's Changes* (Cambridge, MA: Wesley-Addison, 1933), 128.

[3] Clinton and Stanley, *Connecting*, 52.

[4] Edwin Friedman, *A Failure of Nerve* (New York: Church Publishing, Inc., 2007), 29.

[5] Bob Buford, *Finishing Well* (Brentwood, TN: Integrity, 2004), 39.

[6] Ibid., 46.

[7] Terry Walling, lecture for the course, "Organic Leadership Development," Fuller Theological Seminary, May 2011.

[8] Dan B. Allender, *Leading with a Limp* (Colorado Springs, CO: WaterBrook Press, 2006), 8-9.

[9] Terry B. Walling, *Stuck! Navigating Life and Leadership Transitions* (Carol Stream, IL: ChurchSmart Resources, 2008), 63-95.

[10] Ibid., 15.

[11] Url Scaramanga, "Willow Creek Repents?" Christianity Today.com, October, 18, 2007, http://www.outofur.com/archives/2007/10/willow_creek_re.html (accessed October 30, 2011).

[12] Ibid.

[13] Ed Stetzer and David Putman, *Breaking the Missional Code* (Nashville: Broadman & Holman, 2006), 48.

[14] Robert E. Logan, *Be Fruitful and Multiply* (St. Charles, IL: ChurchSmart, 2006), 16-17.

[15] Ibid.

[16] Logan, *Be Fruitful and Multiply*, 16-17.

[17] Garrison, *Church Planting Movements*, 45-46.

[18] Robert E. Logan, "Shared Vision and Mission," from from Coachnet, an online teaching website available to students in Logan's classes.

[19] George Patterson and Richard Scoggins, *Church Multiplication Guide* (Pasadena, CA: William Carey Library, 2002), 184.

[20] Alan Hirsch, *The Forgotten Ways* (Grand Rapids, MI: Brazos Press, 2006), 18.

[21] Ibid.

[22] Ibid., 24-25.

[23] Garrison, *Church Planting Movements*, 21.

[24] Joseph Michelli, *The Starbucks Experience* (New York: McGraw Hill, 2007), 2.

[25] Ibid., 4, 14.

[26] Clinton and Stanley, *Connecting*, 40, 46.

[27] Ibid., 42.

[28] Cole, *Organic Church*, 69-70.

CHAPTER NINE

THE IMPLEMENTATION – A FOUR-YEAR PLAN

Cole states that the Church today needs a system that is practical and profound—a system that is significant enough to tap into the Christian's internal motivation, yet simple enough that it can be easily passed on from disciple to disciple.[1]

I am proposing a four-year plan that can be used again and again. Each time the four-year plan is completed and launched again, it will create a bigger momentum of Kingdom growth.

I led the Anglican Mission Canada (hereafter, AM Canada) to launch this four-year plan in 2012 and we completed our first cycle in 2015. With the help of this four-year plan, we reached a Kingdom growth that we had never dreamed of. Our National Leadership Team (hereafter, NLT) decided to launch this four-year plan for another four years, and we believe it will become a movement helping churches to live out Jesus' parable of the growing seed and to experience the power of Kingdom growth.

This four-year plan is a paradigm-shifting and DNA-changing leadership system that is simple, deep, and focused. It is tailor-made to match the Micro-Macro Discipling strategy. Jesus used examples of farming in his parables of the sower and the growing seed in order to inspire believers to be good farmers. It is his hope that believers would use an organic way of farming from the sowing of seeds to the joy of harvest to further his Kingdom. Disciples of Christ need to respond to Jesus' call to be good farmers and to live out these parables, to prepare good soil, and to work hard on all four stages of the growing seed.

Preparation Year: Sowing of Seeds (January 2009 to June 2010)

As part of the year of preparation between January 2009 and June 2010, I took several steps in order to set the stage for the strategy presented in this book. I gathered data by interviewing leaders and conducting surveys; I personally discipled two young men as a testing ground for discipleship; two blogs for daily devotion were launched; and a planning stage was held with the AM Canada NLT.

Interviewing Leaders and Conducting Surveys

This was the first phase of my effort to test whether the Micro-Macro Discipling theory and strategy works. Chapters 1 and 2 detailed my process of personally interviewing several world renowned leaders and collecting 1,179 surveys from Christians from forty-six churches in order to prove the validity of this theory. To my surprise, all of the Christian leaders I interviewed had the same point of view regarding how critical and important the Micro-Macro Discipling strategy is. All of them agreed that the micro stage of the growth of a Christian, particularly daily devotion, is being neglected by most Christians, including Christian leaders. Many of them stated with certainty that this phenomenon is one of the major reasons for the decline of Christianity and the cause of burnout for many pastors and leaders. The four-year strategic plan is meant to restore this micro stage and make daily devotion a lifestyle so that Micro-Macro Discipling becomes a reality and not just a theory.

Discipling Two Young Men

As a testing ground for discipleship using the Micro-Macro Discipling theory, I personally discipled two young men, and focused on their having daily devotion using my first blog, "Devotion on Fire." I wanted to confirm its success before asking others to do the same. It was a very rewarding spiritual journey with two young teens, one of them being my younger son Athanasius. At first I thought three months might be enough; then it extended to one year because they were not able to build up a lifestyle to be with Jesus daily. I eventually discipled them for two years and eight months before passing the baton to the youth pastor of our church, Rev. Joshua Siu. I am thankful that they are two vibrant young leaders in our church as well as leaders in Chinese Christian Mission (CCM) of Canada today. That is truly a leadership growth from micro to macro—from their personal spiritual lives, to the ministry of their home church, to the ministry of the city of Vancouver and beyond.

Launching the "Devotion on Fire" Blog

There are quite a number of daily devotional materials available, but most of them have only a few verses from the Bible each day as well as stories to help the reader to meditate on the Word. Others are study guides designed to teach people more about the Bible. My call to the "Devotion on Fire" blog is to help Christians to have a healthy spiritual diet daily. Those who follow this blog experience a daily intimate personal relationship with Jesus through reading one chapter of Bible each day, praising the Lord through two English and two Cantonese or Mandarin praise songs, and exercising the power of prayer by praying for various people and ministries. So far people from 114 countries have visited this blog.

Planning Stage with the AM Canada National Leadership Team (NLT)

This was perhaps the most difficult and challenging stage of all because if the NLT had not agreed with my proposal regarding the mission, vision, and strategy as well as the four-year plan for ACiC (see Appendix E), then I would not have been able to complete this book. There were four main stages that led to the NLT becoming involved in this strategy planning process: personal preparation, consultations, the NLT planning retreat, and the AM Canada Annual General Meeting in 2010.

The first stage was my own process of committing to daily devotion. Before I started the Devotion on Fire blog, I was one of the many pastors who did not have daily devotion. Sometimes I used "Our Daily Bread" for two to three days and sometimes I considered my sermon or Bible study preparation as daily devotion. I suffered from the lack of that daily intimate personal relationship with Jesus for years, and I had a few times experienced burnout and had even wanted to quit as a pastor.

The first time I was richly blessed by my new habit of daily devotion was when my wife Michelle was diagnosed with leukemia on April 9, 2010. She was admitted to Vancouver General Hospital the next day with a group of two doctors and four nurses waiting to attend to her immediately. This took place eight months after I had started writing my Devotion on Fire blog and having a daily intimate personal relationship with Jesus. For the first two weeks, I was with Michelle twenty-four hours a day at Vancouver General Hospital, and then Michelle stayed at the hospital for one more week before the doctor sent her home for out-patient chemotherapy. It was the most painful, stressful, and challenging three months we had ever had. Michelle started to have daily devotion with me the first day she was in the hospital.

I remember vividly one day when I was having daily devotion, Jesus said to me, "If you had not listened to me regarding having daily devotion, you would not be able to get through this storm. Without me, you cannot do it." I was shocked and moved at that moment, and I realized that the Micro-Macro Discipling vision I received began with me as the most micro element. From me it also involved my wife, then our two sons, then the AM Canada clergy, leaders, and members, and finally the thousands of other people who are using my blogs and podcasts as a tool for their daily devotion. Without this personal preparation from the Lord, I do not think I would have been able to take up the position of bishop to lead his people.

The second stage of the process involved consultations. I spent almost a year praying, fasting, researching, and analyzing the situation in the AM Canada. Using all I have learned during the five years of my studies from the DMin program at Fuller Seminary, I came up with a proposal for a simple, focused, and deep strategic plan. In hopes that the NLT would accept the plan, I had face-to-face consultations with three DMin professors and church consultants, and during this time the plan was amended before it was presented to the NLT.

On September 13, 2010, I spent two hours with Professor Eddie Gibbs in his home in Pasadena, California. During this time I received important feedback regarding the micro discipleship theory and strategy. On September 15, 2010, I spent three hours with Professor Gil Stieglitz, who had been my personal coach for six years in Sacramento, California. On September 16-17, 2010, I had two full-day coaching sessions with Professor Terry Walling to finalize the plan. Professor Walling commented that he had rarely seen such a concise and practical strategy plan.

The third stage of the process was the NLT Planning Retreat. It was with a frightened heart that I joined this critical retreat at the Everett Hilton Garden Inn from September 27-29, 2010. I worried that the NLT would not accept my proposal for the Micro-Macro Discipling strategy. We had the honor of having Professor Terry Walling as our facilitator to discuss my proposed plan for three exciting days. The NLT had a lot of intense discussion and fierce arguments regarding the plan, and together we produced an amended plan at the end of the retreat. The retreat proved to be very successful in creating a unified spirit within the group, and in creating a revised version of the new vision, mission, and strategy for AM Canada.

The fourth stage was the AM Canada Annual General Meeting in 2010, where the plan was formally approved. The NLT did some detailed planning after the retreat for the upcoming Annual General Meeting (hereafter, AGM). We invited our chairman bishop, the Rt. Rev. Chuck Murphy, to be in this AGM with a special leadership team of three clergy appointed by him. We also planned to hold our first national conference one day after the AGM in order to create a momentum for the Micro-Macro Discipling vision and strategy.

With all the careful planning, the new proposed plan (see Appendix E) was passed unanimously at the AGM on October 29, 2010. The passing of the plan gave us an opportunity to fully implement the Micro-Macro Discipling strategy to all fifteen AM Canada churches. From the visioning and writing of the plan, to the consultation with the three professors, to the involvement of the NLT, to the coming of our chairman bishop's team, to the passing of the plan in the AGM, the process has been somewhat like a mini-version of Micro-Macro Discipling itself—from the stalk, to the head, to the full kernel, and then to the harvest. Once the plan was passed, it felt like a dream come true and the reality of a harvest.

1st Year: The Stalk: "Raising Disciplers" Campaign (September 2010 to August 2011)

During each of the four years of the Micro-Macro Discipling strategic plan, a simple format will be followed for each year. It should be noted that each "year" represents a year on the school calendar rather than a conventional calendar year. First, each September, both the Clergy Retreat and the ACiC National Conference will be held. In March, the yearly campaign will be launched. And in May, the AGM, the ACiC Leadership Breakthrough Conference, and the NLT Retreat will all be held.

Recruiting Coaches on Three Levels

The first wave of creating momentum involved starting first with our clergy. One of the benefits of being a church in the Anglican Mission is that coaching is emphasized. The Anglican Mission provides each bishop and NLT leader with a professional coach. With the extra financial support, it was determined that NLT members would also receive coaching. Professor Terry Walling had been the coach of all five clergy on the NLT for a three-year term. This extra effort to provide a professional coach to all members of the NLT team has proven to be very rewarding so far, as all were being raised up to a new level of leadership.

The second level of coaching is that each of the NLT members will become a coach for two or three senior pastors within our churches. This means that all senior pastors will be coached. The third level involves preparation for coaching other pastors as well as lay leaders in the AM Canada. The NLT leader, Rev. Peter Klenner, and one of the NLT members, Rev. Ed Hird, attended a one-week coaching course with Professor Terry Walling, and they received their coaching licenses as a result. They are equipped to launch a deeper level of coaching for our clergy and leaders. This three-tiered plan for coaching provides our clergy and leaders with a better opportunity to prepare themselves to lead all church members in this movement of MicroMacro Discipling.

First Canadian Regional Conference
(Raising Disciplers, October 15 to 17, 2010)

The Regional Conference titled "Following Jesus" was very successful. This conference created the second wave of momentum for the MicroMacro Discipling movement. Approximately fifty clergy and leaders participated in the conference. The number was not a significant number but it showed a strong start. The success led to the renaming of the conference to "National Conference" beginning in 2011. I had the honor of starting this series of conferences with a keynote talk: "MicroMacro Discipling: Vision and Action of AM Canada." Bishop Chuck Murphy also gave two talks and a sermon, and five different practical workshops were offered by Bishop Murphy's team: the Very Rev. Mike Murphy, the Ven. H. Miller, the Rev. Canon Dr. Allen Hughes, and Mr. Andy Piercy. This conference certainly created a new awareness among our leaders and members regarding the understanding of and the need for Micro-Macro Discipling and the four-year strategic plan.

Launching the Discipler123 Campaign
(March 2011 to May 2011)

The Discipler123 Campaign was launched in March 2011 as the third wave to create momentum for the Micro-Macro Discipling movement. Each member of our churches received a newly designed keyring, one side with the bishop's seal and the other side with the name of this campaign and the sites of my two blogs: "Devotion on Fire" and "Discipler 123." I started to write the Discipler123 blog with English and Cantonese podcasts on March 6, 2011 to create another wave of momentum for the Micro-Macro Discipling movement. The campaign invited people to become disciplers, and to commit to discipling two mentorees for three months. These triads met once a week and encouraged each other to have daily devotion using the Discipler123 blog and/or podcast.

First AM Canada Leadership Conference
(May 25 to 27, 2011)

The first AM Canada Leadership Conference was held in May 2011. This represented the third stage of in-depth training to our clergy and leaders. It also represented the fourth wave of momentum since the four-year strategic plan was launched. We had the honor of having Professor Terry Walling slated to lead this conference for three consecutive years. Approximately seventy clergy members and leaders attended this conference, and all gave positive feedback regarding the quality and practicality of the conference to raise up leaders on a deeper level. The spirit of unity that was experienced by the NLT in September 2010 was again experienced by a wider level of clergy and leaders at this conference. The Micro-Macro Discipling momentum was increased due to Professor Terry Walling's many examples in support of the Micro-Macro Discipling vision and strategic plan.

Second NLT Retreat
(May 27 to 28, 2011)

Following the same pattern of the first NLT retreat led by Professor Terry Walling, Dr. Walling led this two-day retreat immediately following the first Leadership Conference. This second NLT Retreat helped the team to evaluate the effectiveness of the conference and to facilitate the process of planning for the next Clergy Retreat and the Second National Conference in September 2011. This retreat was another valuable opportunity to be with Dr. Walling and to build up team's unity and spirit. At the first NLT retreat in May 2010 the group experienced strong disagreement and scattered visions. At the May 2011 meeting the group was in one accord, working for the same goal through the four-year strategic plan.

2nd Year – The Head: "Raising Evangelists" Campaign
(September 2011 to August 2012)
Clergy Retreat (September 13-15, 2011)

The Clergy Retreat for 2011 was the fourth stage of providing an in-depth spiritual journey for our clergy and the fifth wave of momentum for the Micro-Macro Discipling movement. The retired Primate of the Anglican Church of South East Asia, the Most Rev. Yong Ping Chung, led this retreat titled, "Intimacy with Jesus." It was decided that this retreat would stay on the main focus of Micro-Macro Discipling in order to help clergy and leaders to continuously build a daily intimate personal relationship with Jesus. The clergy in attendance were also encouraged to add to their focus this year the importance of being an evangelist. The group experienced a major breakthrough regarding building trust, team-ministry, and a spirit of unity at this retreat through the superb leadership of Archbishop Yong.

Second AM Canada National Conference
(Raising Evangelists - September 15 to 17, 2011)

Another successful conference—this time the national conference—took place in September 2011. Titled "The Intimate Pilgrimage," this conference created the fifth stage for leadership development and the sixth wave of momentum for the Micro-Macro Discipling movement. Approximately one hundred clergy and leaders participated in this conference, doubling the size of the previous year's conference. This increase in the number of participants demonstrates that momentum had been created. Three world-class speakers were in attendance: the Most Rev. Yong Ping Chung, the Rt. Rev. Todd Hunter, and Dr. Terry Walling. These speakers presented on the practical aspects of the spiritual life and leadership development. I personally led two workshops which were designated for teaching daily devotion using my blogs and podcasts, as well as how to become both a discipler and an evangelist.

The main focus of this second year, evangelism, was introduced by a presentation of Life Transformation Groups, Neil Cole's strategy for discipleship. Cole states,

> The Life Transformation Group (LTG) system is a grass-roots tool for growth. Through this simple system the most essential elements of vital spiritual ministry are released to common Christians without the need for specialized training. It taps the disciple's internal motivation and provides the support needed to grow in the essentials of a spiritual life. The LTG empowers the common Christian to do the uncommon work of reproductive discipling.[2]

This conference created a new awareness for our clergy and leaders regarding how simple and important it is to become both disciplers and evangelists at the same time. The conference created a new momentum that had not previously been seen, which demonstrates the fact that people are being released from maintenance mentality to a genuine revival through the Micro-Macro Discipling movement.

Second AM Canada Leadership Conference
(May 2012)

This second AM Canada Leadership Conference represents the sixth stage of providing in-depth training to our clergy and leaders as well as the ninth wave of momentum for the Micro-Macro discipleship movement. We had the honor of having Professor Terry Walling slated to lead this conference again as a continuation from the previous year's training. This conference provided our clergy and leaders with additional training to build another new level of momentum to the movement.

3rd Year: The Full Kernel: "Raising Mentors" Campaign (September 2012 to August 2013)

Based upon the first two years of hard work using a simple, focused, and deep model to create momentum for the Micro-Macro Discipling movement, this second part of the four-year plan helped us to see the fruits of Micro-Macro Discipling and led us to successfully transition from Micro Discipling to Macro Discipling in terms of mentoring and church planting. Logan offers a good picture of what micro discipling naturally leads to: "The true fruit of an apple tree is not just an apple, but another apple tree. A person can count the number of seeds inside one apple, but only God can count the number of apples inside one seed. Just as disciples reproduce disciples and ministries reproduce ministries, churches reproduce churches."[3] When believers successfully plant an apple tree, then "the true fruit of an apple tree is not just an apple, but another apple tree." Logan calls that "the Creation Principle," and he explains, "It may seem to be a big shift to go from being inwardly focused to being outwardly focused, but it's clearly a biblical one. God will honor a commitment that extends beyond the local church to the universal church."[4]

The Micro-Macro Discipling movement is not an inwardly focused activity but a true biblically based movement, as in the parable of the sower and the growing seed. In Logan's illustration, a healthy apple tree will beget more apple trees. A healthy church will beget more healthy churches. The Micro-Macro Discipling movement will lead to macro church planting. This is the focus of the second part of the four-year plan, and the same simple, focused, and deep pattern will again be used, this time to raise up mentors and church planters.

The third year had the same cycle of preparation for both leaders and lay members. This cycle included the Clergy Retreat (September 2012); the third AM Canada National Conference ("Raising Mentors," September 2012); the second AM Canada Leadership Conference (May 2013); and the third NLT Retreat (May 2013).

4th Year: The Harvest: "Raising Church Planters" Campaign (September 2013 to June 2014)

The fourth year had the same cycle of preparation for both leaders and lay members. This cycle included the Clergy Retreat (September 2013); the fourth AM Canada National Conference ("Raising Church Planters," September 2013); the third

AM Canada Leadership Conference (May 2014); and the fourth NLT Retreat (May 2014).

Conclusion

The implementation of the four-year plan shows how the Micro-Macro Discipling theory has become a reality to enhance healthy growth, and to lead the churches of AM Canada and perhaps your church to a macro level. Each stage has significance in building up momentum for the harvest and cannot be rushed. The plan starts on a micro level and focuses on essential elements which each Christian should be practicing, such as enjoying daily devotion and living out other basic Christian disciplines. The plan then provides a full-scale awakening of the need to raise disciplers, mentors, evangelists, and church planters who will nourish disciples of Christ to live out a relational and missional lifestyle. Cole asserts, "Multiplication may be costly, and in the initial stages slower than addition, but in the long run, it is the only way to fulfill the Great Commission in our generation."[5]

As I am writing this passage, it is now October 2017 and we just successfully completed another National Conference, which we renamed the National Summit three years ago when we started our second cycle of the four-year plan. AM Canada is prepared to put in the time and effort needed to successfully multiply. Garrison also writes, "Rapid reproduction starts with the DNA of the first church."[6] The goal of this strategy is to put the missing DNA, which is micro discipleship, back in its rightful place, and to start with a few or even just one or two churches. Thus, the thirty-fold, sixty-fold, and one-hundred-fold of Jesus' parable of the growing seed may become a reality.

---

[1] Cole, *Cultivating a Life for God*, 36-37.

[2] Ibid., 63.

[3] Logan, *Be Fruitful and Multiply*, 24.

[4] Ibid., 24.

[5] Cole, *Cultivating a Life for God*, 23.

[6] Garrison, *Church Planting Movements*, 195.

CONCLUSION

Two words may be used to conclude this book: "connexity" and "relateonship." Both are new words that cannot be found in the dictionary. "Connexity" is a word that has recently been invented by experts in the business field. "Relateonship" is a word which I have coined in the process of finishing this book. I find that this book started with connexity and completed in relateonship.

Connexity

"Connexity" is a new word being used on the Internet as the blending of the two words, "connected" and "community." Companies like eBay and Amazon.com claim themselves to be in "connexity"—making connections and building communities.[1] In the first and second sections of this book, a connection was made between the Micro-Macro Discipling theory and the discipleship development of the Christian community.

The purpose of this book is to present a mentoring discipleship strategy to develop a relational and missional lifestyle on a Micro-Macro level for churches of AM Canada and beyond. The first section demonstrates the fact that an effective strategy for kingdom development must take into account the uniqueness of the context in which it will be implemented, so this section addresses issues in this aspect. We then explored contextual issues, especially in the reality that fewer than 10 percent of Christians have a daily devotional time, which is directly related to the rationale for launching this Micro-Macro Discipling plan.

The second section describes the biblical, ecclesiological, and theological assumptions that serve as the foundation of the strategy. The book attempts to clarify the goal of the process by asking three simple but basic questions: Why are fewer than 10 percent of Christians having a daily devotional time? Is this a problem? If so, how ought the Church deal with this problem? A theology of Micro-Macro Discipling has been proposed, highlighting biblical teachings regarding the necessity and nature of this strategy.

Connexity is the aim of this book: all data comes together in order to prove the significance of the Micro-Macro Discipling theory for the Christian community. And due to the lack of a daily intimate relationship with Christ for most Christians, clearly Micro-Macro Discipling is truly the missing DNA in discipleship development.

Relateonship

The word "relateonship" is a word which I have coined in the process of completing this book. People rely on many terms and phrases to define different kinds of relationships, such as "acquaintanceship," "apostleship," "apprenticeship," "authorship," "captainship," "chairmanship," "championship, "companionship," "consultantship," "kingship," "lordship," "membership," "mentorship," "professorship," "workmanship," "worship," and many more "ships." We as human beings spend most time of our lives with all those "ships," but not on a daily intimate personal relationship with Jesus, being fully submitted to his Lordship. "Relateonship," then, signifies the fact that we should shift our focus from relating to all those other "ships," and instead relate to the one true one "ship," Jesus Christ our Lord. If we can relate to that "ship," then we should be enjoying the daily intimate personal relationship with our Lord and King.

In this line of thought, the third section provides a practical four-year strategic plan to build up and live out a relational and missional lifestyle on a micro-macro level.[2] The section begins by outlining the tasks of a two-stage simple, gradual mentoring/discipleship process in which people are raised up to be disciplers and evangelists in the first two years, then mentors and church planters in the latter two years. The heart of the proposed strategy is a simple, focused, and deep four-year plan for churches to create a relational and missional Micro-Macro Discipling movement to extend God's Kingdom.

In the process of writing this book, I have received emails of encouragement from various Christian leaders all over the world. Their sharing confirms the importance of this Micro-Macro Discipling vision and strategy. In the past six years since I started to implement the strategy in our churches, I have seen much fruit of Micro-Macro Discipling in my own life and in the lives of others. I have also learned much from those who have shared with me how they are experiencing a daily intimate personal relationship with Jesus Christ our Lord. Many are experiencing a spiritual revival through my blogs, podcasts, and the vision and action of Micro-Macro Discipling.

May Your Kingdom Come

George Barna offers good insight regarding those who would be revolutionaries: "Revolutionaries realize—sometimes very reluctantly—that the core issue isn't whether or not one is involved in a local church, but whether or not one is connected to the body of believers in the pursuit of godliness and worship."[3] I believe that this book is a revolutionary one which may help many churches to go back to their "first love" as described in Revelation 2: 4-5: "Yet I hold this against you: You have forsaken your first love. Remember the height from which you have fallen! Repent and do the things you did at first. If you do not repent, I will come to you and remove your lampstand from its place."

In Acts 19 and 20, the author recounts the establishment by the Apostle Paul of what was perhaps the strongest church in early Church: the church of Ephesus. Paul, in his second missionary journey, started the first training school for missionaries at the lecture hall of Tyrannus. Most of the missionaries in the early Church were from this school. Paul spent three years in Ephesus, and it was the city where Paul spent most of his time.

Many years later, John gave this church at Ephesus a message to call them to repent because they had forsaken their first love. As readers today, it is unknown what really happened at Ephesus, and what John means when he says that they have "forsaken their first love. I would venture to guess that the members of the church at Ephesus had forsaken their daily intimate personal relationship with Jesus, the micro stage of discipleship development. I have seen too many clergy and leaders, including myself, fall into this trap, strategically set by the Deceiver. More study, more work, more service, more "everything" does not help a Christian become closer to Christ; rather doing his Kingdom work and submitting to his Lordship are the keys to deep relationship with him.

It is my sincere hope that this book will stir up a movement of Micro-Macro Discipling to extend his Kingdom worldwide. May his Kingdom come!

---

[1] Robert Lewis, *The Church of Irresistible Influence* (Grand Rapids: Zondervan, 2001), 109.

[2] The idea of "micro-macro" comes from Jesus' parable of the growing seeds in Mark 4:28. If the micro stage ("the stalk") is successful, then a macro effect ("harvest") will follow and there will be thirty-fold, sixty-fold, or even a hundred-fold." Mathematically, one hundred fold is represented by thirty zeros after 1. These four stages (from the micro to the macro level) involve raising up four kinds of leaders: disciplers, mentors, evangelists, and church planters.

[3] George Barna, *Revolution* (Carol Stream, IL: Tyndale, 2005), 38.

APPENDICES

APPENDIX A

Personal Devotion Questionnaire

1. How many day(s) in a week did you have personal devotion in the past 12 months?

    0   1   2   3   4   5   6   7

2. The rate of abundance in your personal life in the past 12 months? (Abundance means a daily experience of wellness in your life)

    0   1   2   3   4   5   6   7   8   9   10

3. How many relative(s)/friend(s) have you brought to our activities/worship in the past 12 months?

    0   1   2   3   4   5+

APPENDIX B

RESULTS OF PERSONAL DAILY DEVOTION QUESTIONNAIRE
FROM A MEGACHURCH

Result of the Personal Devotion Questionaire

1. How many day(s) in a week did you have Personal Devotion in the past 12 months?

	0	1	2	3	4	5	6	7	Total
est.	46	55	38	45	52	50	22	15	323
	14.2%	17.0%	11.8%	13.9%	16.1%	15.5%	6.8%	4.6%	

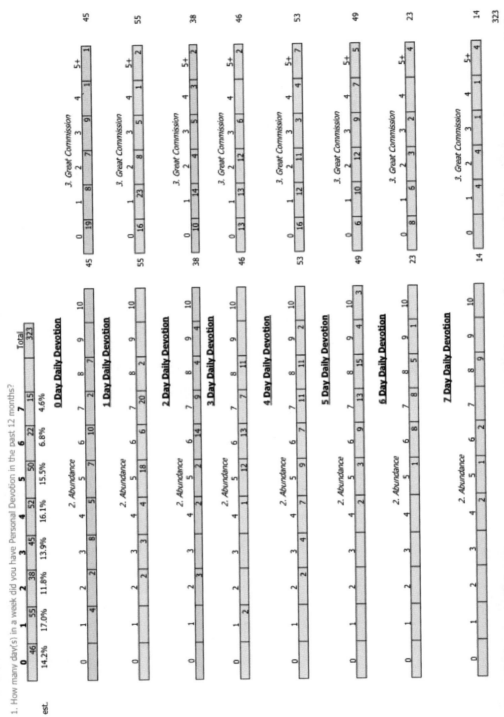

APPENDIX C

1. How many day(s) in a week did you have personal devotion in the past 12 months?

   0   1   2   3   4   5   6   7

2. The rate of abundance in your personal life in the past 12 months?

   0   1   2   3   4   5   6   7   8   9   10

3. How many relative(s)/friend(s) have you brought to our activities/worship in the past 12 months?

   0   1   2   3   4   5+

4. The reason(s) for your daily devotion is because:

   ☐ Guilty   ☐ Duty   ☐ Study

   ☐ Personal relationship with Jesus

Other reasons: _____

APPENDIX D

0	1	2	3	4	5	6	7	Total
57	54	60	44	48	68	43	88	438

0 DAY DAILY DEVOTION

2. Abundance											3. Great Commission					
0	1	2	3	4	5	6	7	8	9	10	0	1	2	3	4	5+
15	5	5	4	2	8	4	5	4	1	2	41	3	8	1		1

1 DAY DAILY DEVOTION

2. Abundance											3. Great Commission					
0	1	2	3	4	5	6	7	8	9	10	0	1	2	3	4	5+
1	9	5	4	6	10	3	6	6	2	2	24	16	7	3	3	2

2 DAY DAILY DEVOTION

2. Abundance											3. Great Commission					
0	1	2	3	4	5	6	7	8	9	10	0	1	2	3	4	5+
1	1	3	7	3	12	6	8	6	1	2	23	14	9	3	1	1

3 DAY DAILY DEVOTION

2. Abundance												*3. Great Commission*					
0	1	2	3	4	5	6	7	8	9	10		0	1	2	3	4	5+
		1	3	5	11	3	5	9	1	2		19	7	10	5	1	1

4 DAY DAILY DEVOTION

2. Abundance												*3. Great Commission*					
0	1	2	3	4	5	6	7	8	9	10		0	1	2	3	4	5+
	1		1	4	4	11	11	9	1	2		12	11	10	7	2	2

5 DAY DAILY DEVOTION

2. Abundance												*3. Great Commission*					
0	1	2	3	4	5	6	7	8	9	10		0	1	2	3	4	5+
			3	3	8	10	17	16	3	3		33	16	13	3	1	3

6 DAY DAILY DEVOTION

2. Abundance												*3. Great Commission*					
0	1	2	3	4	5	6	7	8	9	10		0	1	2	3	4	5+
		1	1	5	2	12	7	4	2			12	9	5	4	2	2

7 DAY DAILY DEVOTION

				2. *Abundance*								3. *Great Commission*				
0	1	2	3	4	5	6	7	8	9	10		0	1	2	3	4	5+
1		1	2	1	10	5	16	21	3	14		28	15	10	6	7	7

Guilty	Duty	Study	Personal relationship with Jesus
35	89	181	342

APPENDIX E

PROPOSAL FOR MICRO-MACRO DISCIPLING

Our Mission and Vision

The Anglican Coalition in Canada (ACiC) is a missionary movement focused on raising up vibrant and authentic Christians through organic congregations and a lifestyle of Christlikeness.

Our Purpose

We exist to empower a fresh expression of Anglicans across Canada who are devoted daily to their journey in Christ and expressing their faith in the living out of the Great Commission.

Our Strategies

The ACiC strategies will always seek to be simple, focused and deep in their impact. The four components of our strategies are the following:

1. Discipling
    Connecting people to God and each other to create a relational climate for raising up disciples and disciplers.

2. Evangelizing
    Creating a climate where disciples and disciplers become missional in both lifestyle and practice.

3. Mentoring
    Providing mentoring and coaching for clergy and leaders to equip and empower them for missional ministry and greater impact in God's Kingdom work.

4. Planting
    The raising up of church planters and new congregations that emerges out of the discipling, missional ministry and the coaching of leaders.

We will provide resources for our congregations and their leaders to live out this strategy.

Four-Year Strategic Plan
(2011 – 2014)

1st Year – The Stalk
Yearly Focus: "Raising Disciplers"

2nd Year – The Head
Yearly Focus: "Raising Evangelists"

3rd Year – The Full Kernel:
Yearly Focus: "Raising Mentors"

4th Year – The Harvest
Yearly Focus: "Raising Church Planters" Campaign

We will organize each year around the following:

1. Anglican Mission's Winter Conference (January or February)

2. Launching of Yearly Focus (January to September)

3. AGM and Leadership Conference (May)

4. Clergy and Leaders Retreat (September or October)

APPENDIX F

How Daily Devotion on Fire helps Christians

June 11, 2010

In the first of Bishop Silas Ng's BLOGs I read, he confessed that even he, a new Bishop, was not faithful to having a daily devotion "every day," and how that is such an impediment to our Christian journey. He acknowledged his own short comings and what we all have to do to be more like Jesus. This was enough to entice me to follow his BLOG every day.

You will find a delightfully candid, enlightened, and wise understanding of the gospel and scripture. Chapter by chapter, in real life application, he teaches with few words, and honest examples.

His 'Daily Devotion on Fire', teaches us how to praise and pray, asks us for prayer, to offer prayer, and to keep praying; to love, to sacrifice and suffer; to listen to and respond to our Lord and Saviour Jesus Christ.

Whether you are a mature or new Christian, familiar with or just starting to know your Bible, you'll find a simple, straight forward method of daily devotion and guidance to a Biblical life and understanding, through a truly intimate time spent with our Lord. The BLOG includes several links to resources and his own instructions for your very own daily devotion.

Thank you Bishop Ng.
David F., ASCC

August 19, 2010

The daily devotion is so complete. Worship music, scripture, reflection, prayer and ending with worship music. Only one I have ever found that is as complete all the while reading the entire Bible.

May God continue to give you the strength and knowledge to continue.

What an inspirational faith builder you are to me.

Blessing,
Anne Harvey

August 20, 2010

Dear Silas,

Happy birthday to your blog.

I have been living with it daily for the past year and has greatly enriched my love for Christ. It has opened a new relationship with him in listening and obeying. I thank our Lord who has given you a great gift to discern His thoughts and boldly teaches us the right things to do. I'll follow you and pray for you and Michelle that Jesus will use you to extend His Kingdom.

In Christ,
S.K.

June 21, 2010
It is all about relationships...

Non believer...dedicated Christian...church goer...crazy lover!

I received Christ about 12 years ago, from an extreme non-believer to a dedicated Christian.

As time went by, my focus shifted away from God. My relationship with HIM has been diminished. I became a church goer. My life was dark and dry. I was self-centered, everything was "me", my egos, my wishes, my problems, my responsibilities.

But **there is a way** and there is a spark...it all happened about 13 months ago at my house group. It began with one question asked by Bishop Silas, "When did you last hear God speaking to you?"I was speechless! It has been so long that I could not even recall! How sad. I was so busy with my life that I could no longer hear Him!

From that day onward, I have decided to rebuild my relationship with God. I started my daily devotion! My quiet time with HIM. Praise the Lord, I fell in love with Him again. The intimacy & sweetness is indescribable & beyond imaginable. HE is my heavenly father, my best friend & lover! It is not easy being a working mom with two kids. Work, kids, school work, chores...can easily drain me out. Life could be miserable, stressful & purposeless. But in HIM alone, I can be refreshed & refueled. HE gives me the **STRENGTH TO LOVE**. The more I love Him, the more I grow to love my family, my friends & colleagues. The more I love Him, the more I am willing to give.

The quality of my relationship to God determines the quality of every other relationship I have! When I'm close to Him, it's easy to be close to others. When I'm disconnected to Him, I'm disconnected to others. could have never experienced this wonderful relationship with God if Bishop Silas has not encouraged me for doing my daily devotion. Everyday I long to be with HIM, to love & to be loved.

In HIM,
Lucy

How Daily Devotion on Fire helps ACiC clergy

August 19, 2010
Rev Ed Hird (Rector of St. Simon North Vancouver, ACiC) said...

Praise God for the 365th Day Anniversary of this Prayer Blog. We have seen many miracles during this time. It has really helped me be more disciplined in my daily quiet time with God, and to encourage my congregation in this discipline.

August 21, 2010

Rev. Edmund (Rector of Toronto Emmanuel Church, ACiC) said...

> Thank you Silas and praise God for this devotional blog! You have set a wonderful example for all of us who are following Christ by having an intimate relationship with Him.

How my 24-hour prayer campaign opens a new door for Christians to understand and practice the power of prayer

August 22, 2010

> Hi Silas,
>
> This is the 17th Saturday morning from 6:00 to 7:00 a.m. as I committed to your 100-day 24 hours prayer campaign, also together with reading your blog. By reading your blog, it encourages me to commit writing to God on a regular basis, i.e. talking to God more intimately and building my relationship with God more closely. Before I was easily disappointed by being ignored. Now, because i have a close relationship with God, I can easily talk to Him (even the whole world ignore me) and hear his response via the bible reading (giving me direction, comfort and strength). I always feel being loved and understood. My prayer time is getting longer and longer.
>
> Blessings,
> Nancy

How Daily Devotion on Fire helps other churches

July 5, 2010

Dr. Paul Huang (A leader in a large Alliance church in Vancouver)

> Dear Silas (if I may call you that as a brother): thank you and the Lord for our divine appointment on our flights home from Calgary; In following your blog/devotion and praying for Michelle, I am glad to read today that she is recovering. Indeed your words of not guilty or duty but the beauty of Christ as the motive for daily devotions that draws deeper dialogue and discernment will be my message to a

class in 2 weeks, while knowing it is a fledgling action even for my-self changing from "regular" to "daily". May the Lord continue to bless you in your dedication and passion in serving/loving Him; blessings, Paul

August 20, 2010

Dear Silas: one day at a time, one person at a time—thanks be to God for our conversation that re-ignited my devotional life and you pas-sion and patience to invest your time in people. It is a small world to have mutual friends like Eddie. Our English adult Christian educa-tion team had a breakfast meeting last week to re-dedicate ourselves to not be just teachers but as shepherds in discipling students but we can't lead where we haven't been ourselves—through daily intimate conversations with God. One day at a time with patience...Leviticus isn't the easiest to plod through...May God bless you, your family and your congregation with much love and joy...and to have more lepers write back. Brother Paul

June 21, 2010
Bishop Thad Barnam
So How's Your Quiet Time Going?

The blog entry below was fun to write. It ends a series of reflections on what discipleship looks like. Instead of taking up the next series I'd planned, I thought I'd spend the next couple of weeks with some personal journaling.

So Erilynne and I were in Denver a few weeks ago. At breakfast with Bishop Silas Ng from Canada we learned his passion for this question about our quiet time with the Lord. He was very clear about it: Most Christians don't do it. He had statistics. Compelling research. With-out personal time with Jesus, he told us, everything breaks down. Church. Ministry. Mission to the world. Everything.

He was not talking about church-attenders. He was talking Chris-tians. Born again by the Holy Spirit. Confessing Jesus as their Lord. The percentage who read their Bible, pray and make intentional time with the Lord is simply low. Really low when asked: Do you do it daily? A little higher when asked: What about several times a week? What about weekly. Just a little. This is it! he said, this declares the poverty of the church! He wasn't done. He had no interest in people who raise their hand and say: I do my quiet time! He said there is a great danger in legalistic duty. Or doing it out of guilt. Or a form of good works that earns God's favor and allows us to wrongfully boast to others. He's talking right desire: It's all about a relationship with Jesus!

I was moved by this. So this past Sunday I preached on a text from Luke 5:16: "But Jesus Himself would often slip away to the wilderness and pray." I love this passage because it is clear that our Lord is way-too-busy. The news of Him has gone everywhere. The sick are coming to Him in droves. And yet He knew boundaries. He knew when to close the door. To stop His work to others. To leave the 70 and the 12. And then "slip away" to be with His Father. Because He wanted to. He needed to. After all, He was and is our High Priest. And His first work as High Priest is to minister to the Lord. To be in His presence and fellowship. The same goes for us who are called a "royal priesthood."

Hard to argue: "I'm just too busy. I have no time." Although I know it's hard. For parents with young kids. For those working long hours, who need quality family time, who need personal time. Where does it fit?!?

I actually found it hard to talk about. I didn't want people to do it because we're supposed to do it. Like a husband who knows he really should bring home flowers to his wife because that's what husbands do. Catch the sermon and tell me what you think:
http://www.apostlesct.org/?q=Podcast
So how's your quiet time?

How Daily Devotion on Fire helps a Christian leader in Hong Kong to become a online discipler

June 21, 2010

Dear Silas,

May the peace of the Lord be with you and Michelle! I've been reading your blog everyday and praise be to God for his rich blessings showered upon you and Michelle.

Actually I'd like to have a quick word with you to share my joy - I felt greatly moved by God on 1st June to read John as my daily devotion and start writing my spiritual journal in Chinese, to share them via email with my godchildren. This is really a great challenge for me for I've always been doing it in English, and writing it in Chinese is real difficult for me. But then, feeling the great urge, and also being moved by your persistence in writing your spiritual journal on your blog daily, I decided to faithfully do it. Today is 21st June and I finally managed to complete this 'task' and I am so happy about it! (God has given me the instruction to continue doing so, but this time to do it with my godchildren, as a mentor to encourage them to do daily devotion together each day. Meanwhile, 5 of them are willing to commit to doing it together with me in the upcoming 20 days. I'm sure God will continue to lead us.)

God bless!

In Christ,
Alice

APPENDIX G

MICRO-MACRO DISCIPLING MODEL

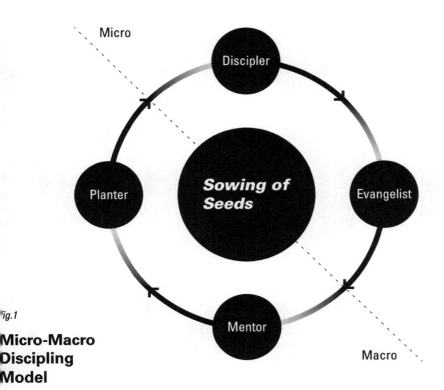

fig.1

**Micro-Macro
Discipling
Model**

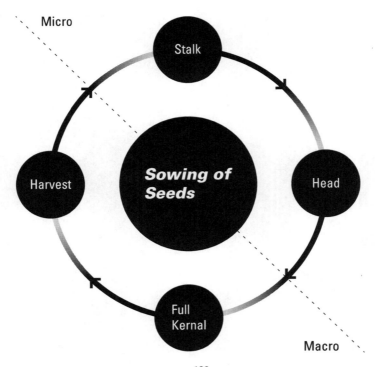

BIBLIOGRAPHY

Allen, Roland. *Missionary Methods: St. Paul's or Ours?* Grand Rapids: Eerdmans, 1962.

_____. The *Spontaneous Expansion of the Church*. Grand Rapids: World Dominion Press, 1962.

Anderson, Ray S. *An Emergent Theology for Emerging Churches*. Downers Grove, IL: InterVarsity Press, 2006.

Balcher, Jim. *Deep Church*. Downers Grove, IL: InterVarsity Press, 2009.

Barna, George. *Revolution*. Wheaton, IL: Tyndale House, 2005.

Barnum, Thaddeus. *Never Silent*. Colorado Springs: Eleison Publishing, 2008.

Barrett, Lois Y., et al. *Treasures in Clay Jars*. Grand Rapids, MI: Eerdmans, 2004.

Borlase, Craig. *The Naked Christian: Getting Real with God*. London: Hodder and Stoughton, 2001.

Breen, Mike and Walt Kallestad. *The Passionate Church*. Colorado Springs: Cook Communications, 2005.

Brewin, Kester. *Signs of Emergence*. Grand Rapids: Baker, 2007.

Buford, Bob. *Finishing Well*. Brentwood, TN: Integrity, 2004.

Carson, D. A. *Becoming Conversant with the Emerging Church*. Grand Rapids: Zondervan, 2005.

Campbell, Jonathan. *The Way of Jesus*. San Francisco: Jossey-Bass, 2005.
Chaney, Charles. *Church Planting at the End of the Twentieth Century*. Wheaton, IL: Tyndale, 1991.

Clark, Andrew, ed. *Encounter with God: Daily Devotion Series*. Pickering, ON: Scripture Union, 2008-2009.

Clifton, Donald and Paula Nelson. *Soar with Your Strengths*. New York: Dell, 1992.

Cloud, Henry and John Townsend. *How People Grow*. Grand Rapids: Zondervan, 2001.

Cole, Neil. *Cultivating a Life for God*. St. Charles, IL: Church Smart, 1999.

_____. *Organic Church*. San Francisco: Jossey-Bass, 2005.

_____. "Paul's Missionary Strategy." Coachnet, website developed by Robert E. Logan for students in his courses.

Drane, John. *Celebrity Culture*. Edinburgh: Rutherford House, 2005.

_____. *The McDonaldization of the Church*. London: Darton, Longman & Todd, 2005.

Drane, Olive Fleming. *Clowns, Storytellers, Disciples*. Oxford: The Bible Reading Fellowship, 2002.

Ferguson, Dave and Jon Ferguson. *Exponential*. Grand Rapids: Zondervan, 2010.

Fitch, David E. *The Great Giveaway: Reclaiming the Mission of the Church*. Grand Rapids: Baker Books, 2005.

Foster, Richard J. *Life with God*. New York: Harper Collins, 2008.

Frost, Michael. *Exiles: Living Missionally in a Post-Christian Culture*. Peabody, MA: Hendrickson, 2006.

Frost, Michael and Alan Hirsch. *The Shaping of Things to Come*. Peabody, MA: Hendrickson, 2003.

Garner, Martin. *A Call for Apostles Today*. Cambridge: Grove Books, 2007.

Garrison, David. *Church Planting Movements*. Bangalore, India: WIGTake, 2004.

Gibbs, Eddie. *Church Morph*. Grand Rapids: Baker Academic, 2009.

_____. *Church Next*. Downers Grove IL: InterVarsity Press, 2000.

_____. *Leadership Next*. Downers Grove, IL: InterVarsity Press, 2005.

Gibbs, Eddie and Ryan K. Bolger. *Emerging Churches*. Grand Rapids: Baker, 2005.

Guder, Darrell L. *The Continuing Conversion of the Church*. Grand Rapids: Eerdmans, 2000.

Hawkins, Greg L. and Cally Parkinson. *Follow Me: What's Next for You?* Barrington, IL: Willow Creek Resources, 2008.

_____. *Reveal: Where are you?* Barrington, IL: Willow Creek Resources, 2007.

Hefling, Charles and Cynthia Shattuck, eds. *The Oxford Guide to the Book of Common Prayer*. Oxford: University Press, 2006.

Herrington, Jim, Robert Creech, and Tricia Taylor. *The Leader's Journey*. San Francisco: Jossey-Bass, 2003.

Hesselgrave, David J. *Planting Churches Cross-Culturally*. Grand Rapids: Baker Academic, 2000.

Hettinga, Jan David. *Follow Me*. Colorado Springs: NavPress, 1996.

Hirsch, Alan. *The Forgotten Ways*. Grand Rapids: Brazos Press, 2006.

Hunsberger, George R. et al. *Church between Gospel and Culture*. Grand Rapids: Eerdmans, 1996.

Hunter, George G. *The Celtic Way of Evangelism*. Nashville: Abingdon Press, 2000.

Jamieson, Alan. *A Churchless Faith*. London: SPCK, 2002.

Jamieson, Alan, Jenny McIntosh, and Adrienne Thompson. *Church Leavers*. London: SPCK, 2005.

Keel, Tim. *Intuitive Leadership*. Grand Rapids: Baker, 2007.

Kimball, Dan. *The Emerging Church*. Grand Rapids: Zondervan, 2003.

Logan, Robert E. *Be Fruitful and Multiply*. St. Charles, IL: ChurchSmart, 2006.

_____. *Beyond Church Planting*. St. Charles, IL: ChurchSmart, 2005.

_____. "Facilitate Churches to Plant Churches – Guide 91." Coachnet, website developed by Robert E. Logan for students in his courses.

_____. "Healthy Church Multiplication." Coachnet, website developed by Robert E. Logan for students in his courses.

_____. "Shared Vision for Church Multiplication Movements." Coachnet, website developed by Robert E. Logan for students in his courses.

Lewis, Robert and Rob Wilkins. *The Church of Irresistible Influence*. Grand Rapids: Zondervan, 2001.

McIntosh, Gary and Samuel Rima. *Overcoming the Dark Side of Leadership*. Grand Rapids: Baker, 1997.

McLaren, Brian. *Finding Our Way Again*. Nashville: Thomas Nelson, 2008.

McNeal, Reggie. *A DVD Curriculum for the Present Future*. San Francisco: Jossey-Bass, 2006.

_____. *The Present Future*. San Francisco: Jossey-Bass, 2003.

_____. *Revolution in Leadership*. Nashville: Abingdon, 1998.

_____. *A Work of Heart*. San Francisco: Jossey-Bass, 2000.

Moynagh, Michael. *Emerging Church Introduction*. Oxford: Monarch, 2004.

Ogden, Greg. *Discipleship Essentials*. Downers Grove, IL: InterVarsity Press, 2007.

_____. *Transforming Discipleship*. Downers Grove, IL: InterVarsity Press, 2003.

Olson, David T. *The American Church in Crisis*. Grand Rapids: Zondervan, 2008.

Pagitt, Doug. *Church ReImagined*. Grand Rapids: Zondervan, 2003.

Patterson, George and Richard Scoggins. *Church Multiplication Guide*. Pasadena, CA: William Carey Library, 2002.

Peace, Richard. *Contemplative Bible Reading*. Colorado Springs: Nav Press, 1998.

Quinn, Robert. *Deep Change*. San Francisco: Jossey-Bass, 1996.

Petterson, Ben. *Deepening Your Conversation with God*. Minneapolis: Bethany House, 1999.

Rah, Soong-Chan. *The Next Evangelicalism*. Downers Grove, IL: InterVarsity Press, 2009.

Roof, Wade. *Spiritual Marketplace: Baby Boomers and the Remaking of American Religion*. Princeton: Princeton University Press, 1999.

Roxburgh, Alan J. *The Sky Is Falling*. Eagle, ID: ACI Publishing, 2005.

Roxburgh, Alan J., and Fred Romanuk. *The Missional Leader*. San Francisco: Jossey- Bass, 2006.

Schwarz, Christian A. *Color Your World with Natural Church Development*. St. Charles, IL: Church Smart Resources, 2005.

Silvoso, Ed. *That None Should Perish*. Ventura, CA: Regal, 1994.

Stanley, Paul D. and Robert J. Clinton. *Connecting: The Mentoring Relationships You Need to Succeed in Life*. Colorado Springs: NavPress, 1992.

Stetzer, Ed and David Purman. *Breaking the Missional Code*. Nashville: Broadman & Holman, 2006.

Stott, John. *John Stott: The Last Word*. Milton Keynes, UK: Authentic Media, 2008.

_____. *The Message of Acts*. Leicester, UK: Inter-Varsity Press, 1990.

_____. *The Radical Disciple*. Downers Grove, IL: Inter Varsity Press, 2010.

_____. *Through the Bible through the Year*. Oxford: Candle Books, 2006.

Sweet, Leonard. *AquaChurch: Essential Leadership Arts for Piloting Your Church in Today's Fluid Culture*. Loveland, CO: Group Publishing, 1999.

Sykes, Stephen, John Booty, and Jonathan Knight. *The Study of Anglicanism*. London: SPCK, 1988.

Taylor, Steve. *The Out of Bounds Church*. Grand Rapids: Zondervan, 2005.

Torrance, Thomas. *Incarnation: The Person and Life of Christ*. Downers Grove, IL: IInterVarsity Press, 2008.

Towns, Elmer and Douglas Porter. *Churches that Multiply.* Kansas City, MO: Beacon Hill, 2003.

Wilkes, Gene. *Jesus on Leadership*. Wheaton, IL: Tyndale, 1999.

Willard, Dallas. *The Divine Conspiracy*. New York: Harper One, 1997.

_____. *The Great Omission*. New York: Harper SanFrancisco, 2006.

_____. *Hearing God*. Downers Grove, IL: InterVarsity Press, 1999.

_____. *Renovation of the Heart*. Colorado Springs: Nav Press, 2002.

_____. *The Spirit of the Disciplines*. New York: Harper SanFrancisco, 1988.

Wright, N. T. *New Testament Devotional Commentaries Series for Everyone*. London: John Knox Press, 2008.